BEECHWOODS
& BAYONETS

THE BOOK OF HALTON

FRONT COVER — LEFT: The badge of Royal Air Force Halton. Its early military origins are recalled by the wooden propellor and its Rothschild associations by five barbed arrows. The latter are taken from the Rothschild coat of arms and represent the five sons of the family's founder. The surrounding laurel wreath denotes excellence in the work of the five Service units housed at RAF Halton and the motto TEACH LEARN APPLY signifies their role in training as well as other functions. (Reproduced by courtesy of the Station Commander); RIGHT: snapshot of Alfred Rothschild taken at a Halton party and BELOW: Halton House today.

A peaceful canal-side scene in Halton. Order and neatness were a feature of
this model village. (ER)

BEECHWOODS & BAYONETS:

THE BOOK OF HALTON

BY

ANDREW E. ADAM

BARRACUDA BOOKS LIMITED
BUCKINGHAM, ENGLAND
MCMLXXXIII

PUBLISHED BY BARRACUDA BOOKS LIMITED
BUCKINGHAM, ENGLAND

PRINTED BY
HOLYWELL PRESS LIMITED
OXFORD, ENGLAND

BOUND BY
GREEN STREET BINDERY LIMITED
OXFORD, ENGLAND

JACKET PRINTED BY
CHENEY & SONS LIMITED
BANBURY, OXON

PHOTOLITHOGRAPHY BY
SOUTH MIDLANDS LITHOPLATES LIMITED
LUTON, ENGLAND

DISPLAY SET IN BASKERVILLE
AND TEXT SET IN 10½/12PT BASKERVILLE BY
BEDFORDSHIRE GRAPHICS LIMITED
BEDFORD, ENGLAND

ISBN 0 86023 183 6

Contents

Foreword

by Mr Bob Grace

To one born within sight of Halton Woods, whose family were tenants at the Halton mill during the 18th century, an authoritative history like this with its fabulous stories of the Rothschild era at Halton fulfils a longstanding need.

The author recounts with admirable clarity and impartiality the events which brought forth the Halton of today from its past splendours. In his later chapters he tells how Halton went to a war that Alfred Rothschild and his brothers had tried to avert.

My own earliest memories are of those Great War soldiers of whom Dr Adam writes. Some were billetted in our home, where they seemed very large to a small boy. They spoke with strange accents and played with my toy football. One day they invited us to come to where the golf course now stands. The soldiers had dug a sap to mine some practice trenches and it was on the point of being blown up. In my memory I can still see the earth and smoke rising in a great mushroom cloud.

Later, my family were heartbroken at the felling of the beautiful Halton beechwoods, which went for duckboards for the trenches. I was too young to realise that, as the trees fell, so did my soldier friends of the Northumberland Fusiliers, none of whom survived. As the poppies covered the Flanders fields, so did rose-bay cover the Halton hills. For years the scarlet flowers drew country lovers there, who did not remember the autumn tints of the beechwoods under which we used to shelter.

Preface

R. G. Grace.

by Air Vice Marshal John N.C. Cooke

Andy Adam worked until recently as a doctor in the RAF at Halton, where he became an accredited specialist in two subjects — those of histopathology and Alfred Rothschild. As a medical colleague I can bear witness to his prowess in the former interest; as to the latter, this book will confirm the amount of detail he has culled from his researches. These have resulted in the marvellous collection of photographs reproduced herein, together with an authentic account of the Rothschild era at Halton which, if it dispels some of the favourite myths, has replaced them with even more entertaining facts of a life-style totally divorced from that of the present occupants of Halton House. Nevertheless, the fascination of those times lives on in the whole area and particularly in the house, which I first saw in 1935 as a teenager, when my father was posted to Halton and when the RAF was still 'the best flying club in the world'. Within a year that phase ended in its turn, as RAF Halton played its part in the urgent expansion of the RAF before the Second World War.

With many others I have several times heard Andy give his public (and private) talks on local history and the the Rothschilds. It seemed entirely appropriate when he bought his house and the Halton Village Post Office opposite the Church. Now that he is leaving the area, both his friends and audiences will be grateful that he has decided to write this book, which will be a continuing pleasure for all of us.

Acknowledgements

When the evening sun strikes the gilded ceilings of Halton House at a certain angle, the rooms dazzle with a Midas touch and the talk turns naturally to Alfred de Rothschild. One evening in the mid-1970s, during a recitation of particularly scandalous fiction, it became clear to several officers around the bar that here was a rich vein for proper historical research.

Chronologically therefore my first acknowledgement is to those RAF colleagues with whom I collaborated briefly before the vagaries of Service life separated us: Group Captain Peter Clifford (retired), Wing Commander Tony Cullen, Squadron Leader Ian Hill, Mrs Monica Harries and others. Their labours I have gratefully incorporated in my own. To the late Reverend (Wing Commander) Douglas Northridge, who had a deep and reciprocated love for Halton village, this book owes a great deal. His encouragement and enthusiasm gently urged the manuscript beyond the point of no return.

As the scope of the project widened so did its debt to others. That debt extends gratefully to my old mentor, Dr Roger Highfield of Merton College, Oxford for advice on primary sources; staff at the Aylesbury County Library, Buckinghamshire County Records Office, the County Museum, the Bodleian, the British Museum and Wendover Library; Mr Bob Grace and the late Mr Hayward Parrott for generous assistance from their detailed local knowledge and for loans from their personal photographic collections; Miss Monica Dunbar for fascinating material produced from unlikely sources; the late Mrs Elizabeth de Rothschild for material from the family library; staff at the National Gallery, Christies, the Wallace Collection and the Courtauld Institute of Art for details on Alfred Rothschild's art collection; the British Architectural Library for details on the building of the chateau; Mr Donald Bassett of Edinburgh University for architectural commentary; the National Monuments Record for making available some beautiful and unpublished Bedford Lemère photographs; the *Buckinghamshire Herald* for letting me scrutinise several decades of back numbers; my friend and colleague Mr Norman Chandler for invaluable help with the illustrations, the steady hand of my father, Dr Robert Adam, for the floor plan of the chateau in chapter 3, and Squadron Leader John Kershaw for the specially drawn endpaper sketches.

Although this study had no official backing, I received much useful help from the Air Historical Branch of the Ministry of Defence, the Adastral Library, various other Service departments and the Imperial War Museum. Successive presidents of the Halton House Mess Committee have allowed me to study the Mess records and reproduce photographs, and successive officers commanding the Administrative Wing at RAF Halton have permitted similar liberties with the station records.

The narrative also owes much to groups of people too numerous to mention by name. They include a large number of elderly Buckinghamshire residents (many of them the children of Rothschild employees), whose vivid recollections of the early 1900s gave substance to the bones of the Halton story, and to the Great War veterans who have set down their reminiscences of Halton during its painful transformation between 1914 and 1918. I am particularly grateful to Mrs Alice Kirsop, niece of Private Arthur Patrick of the Northamptonshire Regiment and two Australian Flying Corps veterans, Sir Ronald East and the late Mr Eric Bowden, who sent unique material all the way from Australia. Finally I salute with thanks a number of retired Royal Air Force officers stationed at RAF Halton during the 1920s and 1930s. Chief among them are Mr Peter Stainer, Group Captain Tom Nicholls, Group Captain Stuart Carslaw and Air Vice Marshal Ewing. Their recollections were corroborated by the dwindling number of former civilian employees on the pre-war station.

A large number of RAF and local friends have encouraged me over the years, with understandable lapses into scepticism as the project entered its seventh year of gestation. I am especially grateful to those who made publication of this book possible by subscribing and assisting its promotion. They include Wing Commander Jim Beveridge, Squadron Leader Beryl Escott, and Warrant Officer Alan King, and the Buckinghamshire library authority and their management and staff at Aylesbury and Wendover. My thanks go to Mr Bob Grace and Air Vice Marshal John Cooke for writing the forewords. My first and last debt is to my wife Jacqui, who for years has put up with a litter of papers as I struggled for authorship with one hand and professional examinations with the other. There were times when the name of Alfred was more on my lips than was her own, yet she never failed cheerfully to listen, to discuss and retype the pages.

Wherever possible I have sought diligently to give the correct acknowledgement to illustrations. Difficulties inevitably arise where prints exist in more than one collection and I must apologise for any unintentional errors in attributions.

Halton Apprentices' Song

How green are the beeches that grow on the Chilterns,
At Halton, up Beacon, and Boddington crown,
But best I remember when beech leaves were falling
And painting the hillside a deep golden brown.

When beech leaves are falling, are falling, are falling
Wherever I'm stationed, where'er I may roam
Old memories come calling, come calling, come calling,
Of youth's golden scenery, of Halton and home.

Dedication

This is for Jacqui

Introduction

This is the story of how a quiet country estate in Buckinghamshire, no more than an hour's travel from London, became involved in a remarkable series of social and historical events. From obscurity under the Dashwood family of West Wycombe, it was thrust to the forefront of late Victorian society by Alfred Charles de Rothschild, a millionaire playboy and an incorrigible extrovert.

The first part of the story reflects powerful trends in 19th century England: the decline of great county families, the depression in agriculture, the rise of a new commercial plutocracy, and the struggle of the Jews for recognition which was led in Parliament by Baron Lionel Rothschild, Alfred's father. At the turn of the century Alfred flourished at Halton in Byzantine luxury; he burned as brilliantly and vanished as quickly as a meteor. Then the fabric of English aristocratic society melted in the crucible of the Great War and so did Alfred's idyll. When the smoke cleared, the ruined pastures and woodlands of Halton had a less flamboyant owner, the infant Royal Air Force.

The RAF's presence at Halton is as long established as the Service itself, and in sixty years it has laid an infinitely firmer print on the place than the Dashwoods or Rothschilds. But, as Thomas Hardy said, war makes rattling good history and peace but poor reading, so the final chapter is a social account of Halton between wars and not a station history.

The central feature of this tale is Alfred's great chateau, Halton House, and one has to admit at the outset that it illustrates how firmly beauty lies in the eye of the beholder. Even on a brilliant summer day with flags flying from the roof and the gardens ablaze with colour, the chateau still arouses feelings of jaundice as readily as those of joy. The stricture of Sir Algernon West sticks like mud to the stonework: 'An exaggerated nightmare of gorgeousness and senseless and ill applied magnificence'.

Very little has been written about Halton House, and the elderly villagers and Great War veterans who dimly remember the Rothschild era are passing on; they leave a void that fills rapidly with invention. Thus Queen Victoria slept here (untrue): Edward Prince of Wales broke his leg on the backstairs pursuing a maid (untrue — it happened at Waddesdon): chorus girls replaced the marble nymphs on columns in the Italian gardens during stag parties (improbable); Lily Langtry was set up in a chalet in the woods (untrue). Secret tunnels, buried jewels, swimming pool frolics in asses' milk . . . most of it is lascivious conjecture which someone dreamed up in the '38. Even the story of how the Crown gained possession of Halton has been distorted beyond recognition.

The trouble is that to this day Halton House can beguile one into believing such tales. Standing on the balcony above the great salon you can almost hear the echoes of coquettish laughter, the volleys of champagne corks above Hungarian violins, the swish of court dresses and the soft tiptoeing between bedrooms, as rosy fingered dawn lightens over the Chilterns.

This, however, is to surrender to the chateau's spell. At the risk of spoiling the fun before the show has started, I must point out that Alfred's circle were at their most discreet when their behaviour was at its most imprudent. Yet readers, I hope, will find the facts of the story at least as interesting as the fiction, which has not knowingly been included.

A.E.A.

Halton Village

Autumn 1982

ABOVE: Brasses in St Michael's Church, depicting Baron Henry Bradshawe, Lord of the Halton Manor 1545-1553, with his wife and eight children; (AA) LEFT: coat of arms of Henry Bradshawe, Chief Baron of the Exchequer, (AA) and RIGHT: St Michael's Church, Halton, rebuilt by Sir John Dashwood-King (4th baronet) in the early 1800s, probably in grey stone of Denner Hill origin. (AA)

Domesday and Dashwoods

'Beloved, beechy Bucks' — *Benjamin Disraeli*

The origins of the manor of Halton in the hundred of Aylesbury are lost in the shadows of the Anglo-Saxon kingdoms.

It is unlikely that they go back any earlier. There are no Roman remains at Halton and, though there were British hill forts (or Saxon earthworks, according to your fancy) at nearby Beacon Hill and Boddington Hill, both are high on the Chilterns escarpment above the Vale of Aylesbury.

In contrast Halton's location, four miles south east of Aylesbury at the foot of the Chilterns and across the Icknield Way, would have been strategically vulnerable. Moreover, right down to Norman times the Chiltern forest was a hostile hinterland full of wolves, wild boar and less tangible terrors.

During the Anglo-Saxon period Halton may have had some military significance. Lipscomb in *The History and Antiquities of the County of Buckingham* (1847) noted its proximity to the southern borders of Mercia, which was a battleground between the Danes and the Saxons in the 9th and 10th centuries. He speculated that it may have been given to the Church as a result of a pious vow or in gratitude for deliverance.

Whatever the reason, we know that around AD970 the manor was owned by Aschwyn, Bishop of Dorchester, and then bestowed on the monastery of Christchurch at Canterbury, which also owned the manor of Monks Risborough.

Immediately before the Norman invasion, however, it was in the hands of Leofwine, brother of the luckless King Harold. The family had a reputation for encroaching on church lands and it is possible that Leofwine grabbed Halton illegally. In the event he perished with Harold at the Battle of Hastings and the manor was confiscated and bestowed on Llanfranch, the first Norman Archbishop of Canterbury. In 1070 it was restored again to the monks of Christchurch.

The manor of *Haltone* (alternatively styled Haulton, Healtun and Halkhton in mediaeval documents) merited a five line entry in the Domesday Book (1086). The land was assessed at five hides, a variable measure as large as 120 acres, with sufficient arable land for seven plough teams. The lord's demesne maintained two teams and the villeins' five. The manor's population was 10 villeins and 15 bordars, who were one grade up from a serf. At this time the population of the whole shire was only 5,095 persons.

Two further assets were a mill, valued at 15 shillings, and woodlands sufficient to feed 100 swine. Under Edward the Confessor the manor had been valued at £8 a year, payable to the King. By comparison neighbouring Wendover was valued at £38 a year and credited with enough woodlands to feed 2,000 pigs, the largest such assessment in the shire!

After the Domesday survey Halton appears to have remained largely untroubled until the reign of Henry VIII. In 1545, during the dissolution of Church lands, he appropriated the manor and advowson (the right to appoint to the church living) and sold them for 800 marks. The new owner was Henry Bradshawe, a successful lawyer who crowned his career by becoming Chief

Baron of the Exchequer shortly before his death in 1553. His brass effigy, kneeling piously in judge's robes with his wife and eight children, survives in the parish church of St Michael at Halton.

During the reign of Elizabeth I the manor passed to the Fermor family, who farmed it for nearly 150 years. We have few details of Halton's fortunes during that period, even during the Civil War. The tenants, through their lord Richard Fermor, joined in the general protests against Ship Money and later, as an undefended village in a mainly Parliamentary shire, Halton must have had its nervous moments. There was sporadic fighting around Aylesbury between 1642 and 1644; Wendover was sacked by the Royalists in 1643 and again in 1645, together with Stoke Mandeville, Ellesborough, the Kimbles and the Risboroughs.

Perhaps for tactical reasons, Halton's Royalist rector John Latimer was not ejected until the war ended in 1646. But he was back again in 1660 with the Restoration and he was clearly a sanguine character. In 1667 he was in serious trouble for the manslaughter of his servant, Christopher Harper, to whom he delivered a 'passionate and indiscreet correction'. Harper survived the beating by some months, which may have been taken in mitigation, for the cleric was lucky enough to obtain a pardon.

In August 1720 James Fermor sold the Halton estate and manorial rights to Sir Francis Dashwood, first Baronet of West Wycombe, for £19,000. Sir Francis had to raise a sizable mortgage and almost immediately petitioned for a reduction in his land tax, on the grounds that the Fermors, being Catholic, had been assessed at double the normal rate. (The Dashwoods were Protestant).

The modern history of Halton starts at this point; plentiful material survives in the Dashwood papers, including a ground plan of the old manor house. It lay in Halton village, a little west of the church on a site which later became Alfred Rothschild's vegetable gardens. It was a plain rectangular house, about 60 feet square, and according to Lipscomb it had fine views over the Vale of Aylesbury from which it could be seen 'bosom'd high in tufted trees'.

There was nothing else worthy of description. At the rear were barns, sheepcotes, and 'kitchen gardings' — all the practical aspects of a squire's home. In the 1870s the Rothschilds had it knocked down, to the discomfiture (it was said) of a legion of rats.

During the 18th century Halton was a quiet sheep-raising and arable estate of 1,500 acres, far removed from the junketings at West Wycombe, where the second baronet scandalised society with the so-called Hell Fire Club. It was chiefly noted as a pretty village of stone cottages and thatched roofs, leafy lanes and beautiful beechwoods, which provided the Dashwoods with additional revenue. At one point they also supplied oak to the navy yards at Chatham. The rent roll itself was modest: an undated 18th century document shows £385 a year from 17 tenants.

When the second baronet died heirless in 1781, Halton passed to his half brother John, who had also assumed his mother's family name of King by Act of Parliament. He died in 1793, and his son, the second Sir John Dashwood-King (the fourth baronet) inherited. He was to be particularly closely identified with Halton.

In the 1790s the rural peace of Halton was shattered by the arrival of the Industrial Revolution. The proprietors of the Grand Junction Canal Company wanted to push a feeder branch through from Wendover to Marsworth, to supply water to the Tring summit. For a small extra investment they were prepared to make the branch navigable. The excitement these proposals must have generated can be likened to the welcome given to an eight-lane motorway slicing through a national park. After due negotiation, however, Sir John decided to permit the new-fangled device. The navvies moved in, bringing with them all the filth, chaos and destruction associated with their work. Soon Sir John was writing bitterly to the Company's offices with a list of grievances. Besides destroying the millstream and the mill that dated from Domesday, the navvies created the reservoir at Weston Turville and drowned the old road from Halton to Wendover. Mounds of earth and mud were everywhere, Sir John's feudal rights were ignored and the Company was in arrears on rates and taxes. Finally there was the flooding. 'I cannot but draw a very painful inference' wrote Sir John indignantly 'from the circumstance of the lands adjoining mine being drained at the expense of the Company and mine being inundated by the waters of it'!

Nevertheless the work was complete by 1797 and at first the canal fulfilled all expectations. It was down the Wendover branch that Farmer Westcar of Creslow pioneered the transport of cattle by water in 1799. He shipped an ox to the Smithfield Christmas show. Having lost no fat *en route,* the beast weighed 241 stone, took first prize and sold for the remarkable sum of £100.

(Later the fortunes of the Wendover branch declined; it leaked abominably and by 1900 was actually bleeding the main canal of water, rather than supplementing it, so it was closed down.)

Sir John had done well from the canal financially, with the sale of freeholds as well as compensation. It was money badly needed, for he was weaving a web of mortgages and debts which, by the end of his life, threatened to engulf the Dashwood family.

At first, however, all went well with the village. St John Priest in his *Agricultural Survey of the County* (1813) noted that there were five tenant farms and 31 houses at Halton and that the arable and pasture land was let to the tenants in a fair manner 'the good and the bad being parcelled out among them'. Sir John was interested in improving livestock and he studied contemporary essays on the subject. He rebuilt the parish church of St Michael's, Halton, utilising an attractive local greystone which was also used for cobblestones in London. Three of the bells from the old church (made in 1553) were recast and a fourth was added. Sir John also leased the old manor house to a resident rector, Rev Joseph Wells. Wells himself was a parson-squire straight out of a Fielding novel. He had a fine herd of Alderneys, an excellent cellar and a taste for strong ale. He was also not beyond using mantraps to protect his game, as an inventory of household contents proves.

When Wells moved on in 1815 Sir John, now in his 50th year, saw an advantage in giving up the family seat at West Wycombe to his 25-year-old son George, and moving to the smaller establishment at Halton. Thus Halton became until 1849 the home of the senior Dashwood and gained some reflected glory, for Sir John was a magistrate, MP for West Wycombe in nine Parliaments between 1796 and 1831 and an active sportsman.

The pleasant pastoral picture faded, however, as he advanced in years. By the time Victoria acceded in 1837, the Dashwood fortunes were sliding downhill. There was gross financial and administrative mismanagement on the estates, particularly Halton, with frequent resort to mortgages and solicitors. These matters caused an estrangement between Sir John and his son, George Henry, later fifth baronet. In 1848, when the old man's debts were approaching £10,000, they were neither speaking nor writing to each other.

Still the aged baronet clung on. 'I intend to live to ninety', he wrote to a concerned family friend in 1848; 'I beg you not to mention my infirmities till that period shall arrive'. He was 83 at the time, and when he died the next year his son was frantically searching for a purchaser for Halton in the face of bankruptcy.

Sir George found interest in an unexpected quarter — the Rothschilds, a family of Jewish financiers who only two generations earlier had been scraping a living in the ghetto of Frankfurt-on-Main. Nathan Mayer Rothschild (1777-1836) had emigrated to England in 1800; largely through his brilliant opportunism, the Rothschilds had emerged from the Napoleonic Wars as the richest banking family in Europe.

Nathan Rothschild died in 1836, leaving four young sons aged 18 to 28 who, unlike their father, enjoyed spending money as well as making it. What was more, they appreciated that the only road to social acceptance in Victorian England lay through ownership of land.

For some years they had been coming down from London to hunt in the Vale of Aylesbury. In the 1830s the Vale was a wild and thinly populated area. Its centuries-old grass, deep ditches and absence of man-made obstacles made it (as the *Victorian County History* remarked as late as 1908) 'one of the finest hunting grounds in the country — though it rides a little deep in the wet weather'. With the arrival of the railway at Tring as early as 1837 it was possible to get down from London for just half a day's sport. To encourage the Rothschild sons, their mother bought them a cottage and a few fields near Mentmore, soon after 1836.

The brothers tried hunting with the Old Berkeley, but too often there was no scent and the journey from London was wasted. So they set up their own hunt, and immediately found themselves in trouble.

As foreigners, as bankers, as Whigs and above all as supporters of Free Trade, it was inevitable that the Rothschilds should fall foul of the shire's leading landowner, the Duke of Buckingham. In 1845-6 the country was racked by bitter controversy surrounding the repeal of the Corn Laws. The Duke, who was a Tory and a fervent protectionist, stirred up local feeling and obtained the signatures of his tenants and many local squires to warn 'the Hebrews' off the best hunting land.

The Rothschilds, however, used the wisdom of centuries; they merely turned the other cheek and bided their time. Sure enough, as John Fowler recalled years later, there was a break in the ice and soon the brothers were meeting to hunt on his father's farm at Broughton. As their popularity in the shire increased, other independent farmers and gentry defied the Duke and joined the newcomers.

One thing led to another. About this time Mr James James, who was a native of Aylesbury and solicitor to Lionel Rothschild (the eldest of the brothers), advised him to start buying property in the Vale. Land was reasonably priced and of good quality. The other brothers decided to follow suit and concentrate their estates in the locality. Thus began the enormous investment in Buckinghamshire which continued for two generations and of which Halton formed one fragment.

Ironically, the foundations of this investment were laid on the ruin of their old adversaries, the Grenvilles of Buckingham. For years the Duke had been overreaching himself and disaster was predicted from far off. Besides his ruinous tastes in beautifying the great houses at Stowe and Wotton, he had an insatiable appetite for land. This became suicidal when he resorted to borrowing at 5 per cent to buy farms which could not conceivably yield profits at even 2 per cent.

In 1848 the crash came and the bailiffs marched into Stowe. The Duke's treasures — the most magnificent private art collection hitherto found in England — went under the hammer, but the twenty-eight day sale made a paltry sum of under £100,000. Desperately the family resorted to their ancestral acres and, in a series of forced sales, reduced their English estates from 50,000 acres to a mere 10,000 acres.

(There was a happier ending. After the Duke's bankruptcy the young Marquis of Chandos took employment as an estate manager and later as chairman of a railway company. His salary permitted his father to end his days in comfort in the Great Western Hotel at Paddington. Later this enterprising young man managed to recoup most of the family's losses.)

In 1853 Anthony de Rothschild bought the bulk of the Aston Clinton estate adjoining Halton. Lionel acquired various properties in Aylesbury, Bierton and Hulcott. This was only the beginning for, in the years that followed, the watchful James James quietly bought up other former Grenville properties for the family. In 1853 Mayer, the youngest brother, bought 700 acres from the Duke of Marlborough and set about building Mentmore Towers.

The year after the Buckingham crash saw the death of Sir John Dashwood-King and a more modest sale of the contents of Dashwood Manor at Halton. The catalogue of the sale makes a poor comparison with the Grenville treasures. It lasted six days and included a minor Reynolds, 1,200 ounces of silver plate, candlesticks, cutlery and kettles and a library of 1,500 books.

There was also a complete clearance of the household furniture and farm stock, down to *Lot 1183:* Iron grey horse, aged, 'Drummer', and *Lot 1182:* Brindle cow (calf in a month).

In November 1850 Baron Lionel Rothschild entered into an agreement to purchase the Halton estate for £47,500. Virginia Cowles' brief mention of the purchase in *The Rothschilds, a Family of Fortune* erroneously postdates it by twenty years. The transaction ran into legal snags and the final reckoning between the impoverished baronet and the millionaire baron was as disputatious as any modern property deal.

On the one hand Sir George agreed to hand over at completion the net profits derived from the estate during the negotiation. On the other hand Lionel had to pay an additional 3.5% interest on the purchase price during the waiting period.

Such was the practice of the day, but the man in the middle — Dashwood agent Edward Pheby — tried a sharp move for his employers, by claiming an additional 10 shillings per acre of woodland *for the continuing growth of timber* between the date of agreement and the completion.

Naturally this move was strenuously resisted on the baron's side and there followed some delightful hocus pocus, with the lawyers quibbling over gewgaws. What after all was a matter of £227 to the man who had engineered a £20m loan to finance the abolition of slavery in 1833, who was about to float £16m for the Crimean War and whose greatest coup — £4m raised overnight for Disraeli to buy the Suez Canal shares — was still twenty years in the future?

(In addition to their British operations, it has been calculated that during the 43 years that Lionel was head of the bank the Rothschilds raised over £1,000m in loans for foreign governments.)

Nevertheless business is business and 'lawyers' fingers straight dream on fees'. It was not until 1853 that the solicitors were satisfied, the papers signed and Lionel became the new master of Halton.

Modern interior of St Michael's. (AA)

17

'A connoisseur in the art of fine living': this artificial study was made by Downey's, the Court photographers, and presented by Alfred to many of his friends. (EL)

Family Tapestry

'There were few, even of the old county families, whose territorial influence in one particular area was so strong, so extensive and . . . so completely identified with the traditions of the soil.' *Cecil Roth.*

The middle years of Victoria's reign saw a period of great expansion by the Rothschilds in Buckinghamshire, rather like the European scramble for colonies in Africa.

By the end of the century they had accumulated 30,000 acres in the Vale of Aylesbury. They were established in seven imposing mansions in the vicinity: Tring Park (first Lord Rothschild); Mentmore (Lord Rosebery, married to Hannah Rothschild); Aston Clinton (Sir Anthony Rothschild's family); Wing (Leopold); Halton (Alfred); Eythrope (Alice, Ferdinand's sister) and Waddesdon (Baron Ferdinand). They had gained one peerage and married into two others, and had established a succession of local MPs which lasted unbroken from 1865 to 1923. In Nathaniel, 1st Lord Rothschild, they provided a distinguished Lord Lieutenant of the shire from 1889 to 1915.

This is not the place to trace all the threads in the Rothschild tapestry — simply those that relate to the Halton story and the general background to the brothers' acceptance by the shire. The period before 1879 is not well documented at Halton, because Lionel Rothschild never made his home there. As head of the family he was committed to the family seat at Gunnersbury Park, which he greatly embellished, and to the magnificent town house which he built at 148 Piccadilly. Halton seems to have been regarded as an investment and a convenient hunting lodge.

The three brothers continued ardent huntsmen until late in life, apparently undeterred by the terrible fall suffered by Nathaniel, the fourth brother, which left him crippled for life.(Nathaniel moved to France in 1851 where his vineyards near Bordeaux were to make the name Mouton Rothschild hallowed throughout the drinking world). As senior partner at the bank it was Lionel's bad luck to miss the Monday hunt in order to attend at New Court. He found, however, that he could make up for the disappointment by rising at dawn and 'turning out a deer' before catching the fast train to London.

Since hunting was the Rothschilds' entrée to Buckinghamshire society, the famous Rothschild Staghounds are particularly relevant. To the young London financiers with neither time nor patience for the vagaries of foxhunting, the obvious solution was staghunting. By the mid-19th century this ancient and royal sport had become rather adulterated. Red and fallow deer were bred like racehorses and kept in peak condition with their antlers judiciously sawn off. On hunt days they were transported to the meet by cart, given ten minutes' start, and chased to exhaustion over several hours. If things went well, the verderers would round up the terrified animal unharmed, pop it back in the cart and go home again.

While nobody considered the animals' point of view there was some disapproval at the lack of sportsmanship. In the same period the Earl of Lonsdale kept 'bagged' foxes imported from

Cumberland near Tring and curiously enough, like the Rothschilds, he regularly used the railway. He was richly lampooned in a popular verse:

> 'So they dug him [the fox] out, the Earl and the groom,
> The huntsman and whip and the man with the broom.
> The fox and the hounds are at Tring again
> And his Lordship returned by the four o'clock train.'

In 1839 Lionel purchased the deer stock and hounds from Sir Charles Shakerly. The kennels were first at Hastoe, then at Mentmore and after 1877 at Ascott near the deer paddocks. The pack flourished and doubled in size; new blood was introduced from the pick of the British hunts, the Belvoir, Fitzwilliam and Bramham Moor. At the same time the deer were also freshened up, with recruits from the Savernake forest.

The professionalism of the Rothschild staghounds ensured a thoroughly good day's sport and the quarry often ran more than twenty miles in a straight line. The immaculate turn-out of the hunt, with the horses and officials in Rothschild livery and the Barons (who were Joint Masters) ready to pay all the bills, won many hearts. In 1908 a sporting historian recorded with unconscious irony: 'The hunt is immensely popular with the farmers, a committee of whom is in charge of any arrangements for the removal of any wire that exists'.

In 1914 the Rothschild Staghounds was one of only four remaining private stag hunts in the country. Edward VII, succumbing to rising costs and obesity, had himself disbanded the Royal Buckhounds.

While hunting was about the most important thing in life to the hard riding Buckinghamshire squires — 'the sport of kings, the image of war without its guilt, and only five-and-twenty per cent of its danger' — actually *accepting* the Jewish outsiders into the bosom of county society was quite another.

As *parvenus* buying their way into the preserves of the aristocracy, and as city men with no knowledge of agriculture, the Rothschilds were frequently resented and ridiculed. Yet, in a remarkably short time, they had entrenched themselves in the affections of their neighbours and tenants. Just how did this remarkable integration come about?

The answer is not, as has been represented, that they revitalized a depressed agricultural economy with city money and a building programme worthy of the Pharaohs.

On the contrary, the years 1853 to 1874, during which the Rothschilds were establishing themselves in the shire, were part of the last golden age of English agriculture, in which the Vale of Aylesbury shared richly. Long before 1850 the traditional cottage industries of lacemaking and straw plaiting had begun to decline, but this had been more than compensated for by the transition from sheep raising to dairy farming.

London was a huge and growing market for Buckinghamshire's milk and butter, only 40 miles away down the iron tracks. Beefstock grazing flourished as the old Midland Shorthorns gave way to fat red Herefords; livestock markets were regularly held in Aylesbury, exporting both to London and the north. Wages were high, rented grass commanded good prices and the only people who were a regular charge on the Poor Laws were the old and infirm. (All this was in contrast with the chalklands of the Chilterns, best suited to corn. Wages and rents were always considerably lower and the economy vulnerable to marked fluctuations).

Thus the Rothschilds should not be represented as working some kind of an economic miracle. Their achievement was to graft onto the backcloth of quiet mid-Victorian prosperity their own un-English style of benevolent paternalism towards their tenants and employees. Their social and economic philosophy was summarised in the family motto: *Concordia, Industria, Integritas,* an authentic if rather smug Victorian sentiment. It was interpreted as:

> Let Truth and Concord ever be
> faithful friends of Industry.

This paternalism might be expressed in a wholesale manner, as by Mayer at Mentmore and Ferdinand at Waddesdon, by levelling whole villages and rebuilding in modern designs with proper sewage and water supply. Elsewhere the same policy was more selective and involved; the replacement of decaying tied cottages (at Tring, Nathaniel, 1st Lord Rothschild, was credited with over 400 excellent cottages during his lifetime) the rebuilding of tenant farms and farm buildings; the construction of lodges, village halls, clubs — even public houses like the modest *Rothschild Arms* at Aston Clinton or the massive *Rose and Crown* at Tring (built for the servant overflow of Nathaniel's houseparties.)

Frequently the Rothschilds preempted the responsibilities of the local authorities in housing, schools and libraries. Thus the Rothschild primary schools at Halton and Aston Clinton came into existence 10 years before the 1870 Education Act established them nationally. The Infant's School at Aston Clinton had a curious genesis. It was built in 1859 by the indulgent Sir Antony for his elder daughter Constance, at her request, *for her 16th birthday present.* At Halton Alfred also built a reading room, stocked with newspapers and magazines for the villagers' use. Similarly, hospitals were endowed or built, charities supported and local industries forested. The whole tally would (and frequently did) fill an entire book.

The legacy of this building programme is still clearly visible. There are few villages in the Vale which do not have their quota of decorative half-timbered houses and cottages with deep gable ends, tall chimneys and plaster pictures depicting country crafts and seasons, complete with Rothschild arms and monograms. Halton itself was virtually demolished and rebuilt over two generations in this style.

The character of Rothschild paternalism was summarised in an event which took place at Halton in the grounds of the old Dashwood mansion in June 1868. This was the Halton Industrial Exhibition, a sort of miniature Crystal Palace Exhibition. At the time such an enterprise was unheard of outside large cities and it created national interest, especially since it was opened by Buckinghamshire's most famous resident, the Prime Minister, Mr Benjamin Disraeli. The *Times* gave the Exhibition a glowing write-up, explaining that it originated 'in a desire on the part of the family of Sir Anthony de Rothschild to collect specimens of the industry of the residents in a single parish upon their estates'. As Disraeli put it, they were trying to enlarge the old Buckinghamshire image of 'butter, beef and barley'.

The scheme caught the public imagination and eventually fifty parishes took part. Four acres of Halton Park were taken over by marquees to accommodate 3,000 exhibitors, among whom exponents of the dying arts of straw plaiting (into bonnets, boxes and baskets) and hand-made lace were prominent. As Professor Davis wrote in another context: 'It is probably indicative of their [ie the lace and straw industries] former importance that . . . when philanthropic people turned their thoughts to bettering the poor, their minds usually turned to these trades'.

Another Rothschild objective, upon which Disraeli touched in this opening speech, was 'the earnest movement to improve the residences of the working classes, uniting comfort and convenience with economy'. A competition was sponsored by Lady Louise Rothschild to encourage local carpenters and builders to incorporate new building designs in cottages. The emphasis was on interior comforts and amenities rather than appearance. Scale size models were submitted with their full size specifications, and the winning design was later built to order.

The exhibition was a resounding success. On the first day alone, 5,000 spectators paid two shillings a head for admission, and the exhibition lasted six days. On the final day the price was dropped to twopence to allow all the local people to attend. The contemporary reports suggest that about 25,000 people visited the show, which was a large number in those days of difficult transport.

Interestingly too, this exhibition was the forerunner of the long succession of agricultural shows held at Halton thirty years later during Alfred Rothschild's day. We do not know if the young Alfred, now 26 and newly elected a director of the Bank of England, was involved in any way. (It is unlikely, for he was not present at the opening). But perhaps his interest in Halton was already stirring, if only for its proximity to Aston Clinton where he frequently visited his favourite aunt, Lady Louise.

Among the VIPs invited to the opening were Samuel Wilberforce, the Bishop of Oxford, Archdeacon Bickersteth and no less than 23 rural clergy, whose names were set out in the newspaper report. Their presence is an indication of how carefully the Rothschilds had to walk in their public relations, particularly their relations with the Church of England.

In the eyes of many mid-Victorian Anglicans it was an unholy anomaly that, with their new estates, many Jewish families had acquired a variety of parish churches, together with advowsons (the right to appoint to the livings) which often stretched back to the Norman Conquest. Buckinghamshire was not noted at the best of times for religious tolerance — Roman Catholic emancipation had been bitterly controversial — and this unnatural arrogation by the 'sons of Judah' evoked a hubbub of indignation in the shire.

The Rothschilds played their part tactfully and without provocation. No synagogue was ever established at any of the estates, though occasional services, for example, were celebrated at Tring Park. Lionel Walter, future 2nd Lord Rothschild celebrated his *Bar Mitzvah* there in January 1881. (His uncle Leopold, married the previous Monday, walked over from Ascott through deep snow drifts to attend). No scandal concerning church appointments ever touched the family, who appear to have deferred absolutely to the diocese. They went out of their way to cultivate prelates and keep open house for local clergy.

Surprisingly, perhaps, Rothschild culture and liberality really *did* prevail over much Victorian bigotry. Anthony's little daughters became well acquainted with the local clergy popping in at Aston Clinton, and they were able to compose an alphabet in verse of all their surnames. (The Rector of Mentmore was so tickled that he insisted on showing the original to the Bishop!) And Bishop Wilberforce himself, when performing confirmations at St Michael's, Halton in the 1860s, accepted an invitation to stay with Sir Anthony, bringing with him his private chaplain and coachman. He remained a friend of the family after being transferred to Winchester.

Meanwhile the vaults of N.M. Rothschild and Sons continuously poured oil onto ecclesiastical waters. Wherever there was a need — a church restoration, a new organ loft, a distressed clergyman or even a Nonconformist chapel in difficulties — there was a Rothschild ready to help.

Why, one wonders a hundred years later, did they do so much and so readily? Was it *all* genuine philanthropy (of which they displayed much at a national level) and new-found love of the countryside? Or the ingenuous investment of *parvenus,* burying the spectre of the Frankfurt ghetto in a solid rural identity? Were they, more subtly, recreating the pastoral idyll of the 18th century Romantics, with neat villages of rose-twined cottages, where contented peasants touched their caps, where grateful tenants industriously worked model farms, and where the Quality occasionally came to admire and applaud? Whatever the exact motives — and they varied between individual Rothschilds — one thing became clear. When the golden years ended abruptly in the mid-1870s, no farmer in the Home Counties was quite so fortunate as a Rothschild tenant.

A series of disastrous harvests between 1874 and 1882 coincided with the advent of the mechanised farming and railroad freighting on the great prairies of North America. Corn at unbeatable prices flooded the unprotected British market. It was followed, in the 1880s, by cheap beef and lamb in refrigerated containers from South America, New Zealand and Australia. Cheap foreign bacon also glutted London. All this was the bitter harvest of Free Trade predicted by Disraeli back in 1846.

These world forces broke landlords and tenants alike, drove 100,000 farm labourers off the land between 1871 and 1881 and forced massive regrassing programmes. Buckinghamshire farmers knew their share of hard times, though nothing like the abject poverty which gripped the corn counties. The Rothschild estates, however, were to a large degree buffered by banking money. Already Anthony and Mayer had, in the 1850s, defied local practice by keeping their farm labourers employed throughout the winter. Rents were fixed low — good relations being deemed more important than agricultural profits — and in lean years the Rothschilds were able to remit a large part of them. Their policy of farm improvement, drainage and full employment with no evictions continued unabated. Thus the estates were eased without too much hardship through lean times.

By now a new generation of Rothschilds was taking the place of the old triumvirate. Mayer had died in 1874, Anthony in 1876 and Lionel in 1879.

Only Lionel left male heirs: his sons Nathaniel, Alfred and Leopold, who partitioned his property. Nathaniel, as eldest, took Tring Park,* with a lovely 17th century manor house designed by Christopher Wren. Its 3,600 acres just over the Hertfordshire border marched with the estates of Halton and Aston Clinton.

Leopold, the youngest, had already been given Gunnersbury Park. He now also took the property at Ascott, while Alfred became master at Halton.

All three were destined to make their mark as builders and innovators on their estates, but none so spectacularly as Alfred.

---

* Lionel had made this last great acquisition in 1873, purchasing it from the Kaye trustees for nearly £250,000. There is, incidentally, no truth in the popular belief that the house had once been presented to Nell Gwynn by Charles II for services unconnected with the retail trade in soft fruits.

Concordia, Industria, Integritas — Let Truth and Concorde ever be Faithful
Friends of Industry: a bronze medal presented at the Halton Industrial
Exhibition of 1868; it was awarded to the grandfather of Mr Bob Grace for
his fine handwriting. (RG)

Alfred Rothschild posing in the South Drawing Room at Halton House.
(HH)

Mr Alfred

Mr Alfred can best be described as a connoisseur in the art of fine living —
Frances Greville, Countess of Warwick

What sort of man was Alfred Charles de Rothschild, who succeeded in 1879 to the charming Halton estate with its leafy lanes and empty decaying mansion? At all levels of society he was known simply as 'Mr Alfred'. As with most of the British Rothschilds his preferred style was *de* Rothschild, the *von* to which he was also entitled being reserved (until 1914) for German correspondence.

Sixty years after his death, Alfred remains an enigma, a kaleidoscope of glittering poses. Millionaire, playboy, connoisseur, fop, eccentric, friend of princes, pursuer of showgirls, amateur diplomat — these were the faces he showed the world. Unfortunately, though he appears in the memoirs of almost everybody worth knowing (or reading) in society, Alfred himself was totally unliterary. There is no window into his own thoughts.

Great talents, but little application — that would be a fair appraisal. He never held public office, never entered Parliament and was never associated with any great political cause. In the City he was a disappointment and his *Times* obituarist concluded 'The work of the great business to which they [the three brothers] were born seemed little more than a background in his life'. His one important financial appointment outside the firm ended in a ludicrous scandal. The only British honour he received was a modest CVO in 1902, and his prestigious title of Consul General of the Austro-Hungarian Empire was a hereditary sinecure, handed down through the family like an old shoe.

The contrast with his two brothers, with whom he made up — in the delightful *fin de siècle* phrase — 'the three magnificos' was marked. Nathaniel, the first Lord Rothschild, was the full bearded, humourless, well read and extremely well informed eldest brother. Disraeli once remarked: 'When I want to know a historical fact I always ask Natty'. Upon his shoulders rested the House of Rothschild and the leadership of British Jewry, and he bore them like the Rock of Ages.

Leopold, the youngest, was everybody's favourite, immensely good natured and an inexhaustible philanthropist. He was also a passionate sportsman and popular race horse owner; he once remarked that there was only one race greater than the Jews, and that was the Derby.

Surprisingly, Cecil Roth, a leading historian of Anglo-Jewish society, considered that Alfred played a more important part than either of them, and was one of the oustanding (as well as most picturesque) characters of the Edwardian era.

His case is based on Alfred's efforts to mediate privately between the British and German governments to lessen international tensions. It is true that on one occasion in 1898 Halton Mansion was the venue for informal discussions between Joseph Chamberlain, the Colonial

Secretary, and Count Hatzfeld, the German Ambassador, about a possible Anglo-German *entente* which never materialised. For the rest, Alfred's diplomacy consisted mainly of inviting the right people to dinner together, and on the evidence which he produces — or merely alludes to — Roth was straining at gnats. The place of Alfred as a serious Edwardian figure (if indeed he has one) has still to be established.

Our concern, however, is not with historical reputations but with the tastes and ambitions which led Alfred into his Halton venture. Fortunately these are well documented by critics of all shades.

In 1879 Alfred was already 35 years old, an age at which most Victorian sons were content to settle down and beget large families. He was, and remained for many years, one of London's most eligible bachelors. Not only was he incalculably rich, but he possessed all the looks and graces necessary to succeed in Society. He was an elegant little man, short, blond and handsome. In youth he cultivated dundrearies, but later adopted dashing 'favoris' which his personal barber trimmed meticulously for him.

A typical English upper class education (King's College, London and Trinity College, Cambridge) had given him the polished self-assurance which — combined with his wealth — captivated women, from duchesses to girls in the chorus line. The intriguing thing is that he did it without necessarily making enemies of their husbands.

At New Court, the head offices of N.M. Rothschild and Sons, he was an able but erratic partner, who always insisted on taking Fridays off to get a good start to his weekends — a practice which would have horrified his grandfather. When he did work, he usually arrived as late as 2.00 pm, lunched between 3.30 and 4.00 and settled down to a nap around 5.00, when his brothers departed. This presented the long-suffering staff with a tactical problem, for a partner's signature was required on the day's correspondence. The problem could be solved by dropping a copy of *Kelly's Directory* outside the partners' room with a crash that restored Alfred to productivity.

Alfred's dilettante attitude toward business was vividly demonstrated in his directorship of the Bank of England. In 1868 the Bank felt it politic to strengthen its ties with the Rothschilds, and Alfred had the distinction of becoming (by family selection) the first Jewish director of the Bank at the youthful age of 26. For twenty years he served at Threadneedle Street and was reelected time after time. But in 1889 (so the story goes), he bought a certain expensive French painting from a dealer. A gnawing suspicion took hold that he might — for once — have been outsmarted. It turned out the dealer had a Bank of England account, so Alfred sneaked a quick look. It proved his undoing. The dealer's profit was nothing short of scandal, but nothing as big as the scandal which resulted when Alfred blabbed of it. His resignation then became unavoidable.

The truth was that Alfred had a far greater gift for spending money than for making it. Fine paintings, furniture, porcelain, jewels, the company of beautiful women, music, clothes and luxuries of every description were his love and joy. His most abiding passion was for paintings and, whatever his detractors said about his architectural tastes, his artistic sense was acknowledged as superb.

Thus, though many Rothschilds were celebrated as collectors, Alfred was the only real *connoisseur*. Lady Dorothy Neville described him as the finest amateur judge in England of the 18th century French school, as well as a great connoisseur of the English and Dutch schools. He was a collector on an epic scale.

With the help of Charles Davis, the Bond Street dealer who published the catalogue of his paintings in 1884 (of which a copy survives in the Victoria and Albert Museum library), he built up superb collections, first at his London home, 1 Seamore Place in Mayfair, then at Halton. Porcelain and Sèvres china were two other passions. Unlike Mayer, who had spent a fortune amassing the Mentmore collection in a relatively short time, Alfred was a life-long collector. As late as 1917, shortly before his death, he bought a Titian, *Allergory of Prudence,* which is now in the

National Gallery. Alfred became a trustee of the National Gallery in 1892 and of the Wallace Collection in 1897, and fulfilled both duties conscientiously. More than once he supplemented meagre Government grants to prevent important acquisitions being lost. His exasperation with Sir Charles Holroyd, the director of the National Gallery, for refusing a particularly fine Raphael on the grounds of *cost* without first consulting the trustees boiled over into the *Times* correspondence columns.

Besides art he adored music, especially grand opera, and of course he had a box at Covent Garden. During the season he cultivated the celebrities and threw magnificent receptions for them at Seamore Place. The musical content of these glittering evenings became famous in London society. As we shall see, Halton shared in the glitter.

Alfred also loved theatre and was an inveterate first nighter; Disraeli frequently sought his advice on matters of entertainment. He was patron of such lovely and mercenary ornaments of the stage as Lily Langtry. When the impresario George Edwardes persuaded him to take over the Gaiety Theatre, Alfred had an entrance into the colourful world of Victorian musical comedy. There is no doubt that he put ambitious thoughts into many a pretty head, for Edwardes' Gaiety Girls had a formidable track record in the so-called 'actressocracy' stakes. Successful runners included the Countess Ostheim, Countess Torrington, Lady George Cholmondely, the Countess of Suffolk, Lady Churston, Lady Victor Paget, the Countess Poulett and the Marchioness of Headfort. Finally Edwardes had to put a clause in his artistes' contracts banning their release for matrimony during the running of a show.

Millionaire, connoiseur, man-about-town — in all roles his contemporaries agreed one thing. Alfred de Rothschild was a man of princely bounty. Lady Neville wrote of his superb 'generosity and kindness of heart both in his personal relations and towards charities'. He not only drained the cup of life to its dregs but he derived his greatest pleasure from charging and recharging it lavishly for the enjoyment of his friends.

Who else but Alfred Rothschild, one wonders, could have needed — or afforded — the £1,000 sent round from the bank in freshly minted notes to Seamore Place every Friday for his weekend spending money?

Later, of course, as the aging playboy moved from his sixth to his seventh decade, the dashing aura faded. With no wife to cosset him and with an obscure dyspepsia and cardiac condition to plague him, Alfred was at the mercy of his servants and physicians. He grew into an hypochondriac, the butt of wags like Max Beerbohm, and at times must have appeared to be supporting Harley Street single handed.

In town a fashionable physician called daily to assure him that he was in good health, and in the country his personal doctor and nurses were in constant attendance. At Halton the number and variety of bottles in the medicine chest rivalled those in the cellars; disaster once struck when a cherished pet dog gulped down some of Mr Alfred's heart pills and promptly expired on the carpet.

He sought the ultimate refuge of the neurotic, surrounding himself socially with surgeons and physicians as friends. They included Sir Milsom Rees (who was also one of his executors), the celebrated and Royal laryngologist who knew more than anyone alive about the mysteries of the vocal cords; like Alfred he was a frequent attender at the Royal Opera House, where he had an honorary appointment. Sir Francis Laking was another familiar. As a Household Physician he was on intimate terms with the workings of the Royal viscera, which was a great comfort. The young Bertrand Dawson — later Lord Dawson of Penn — was another Royal surgeon whom Alfred befriended. Rees and Dawson both profited from Alfred's will, Dawson being bequeathed £25,000 for a trust fund from which to help patients who urgently needed treatment beyond their means.

27

But in 1879 these doleful changes were well in the future. In 1879 Alfred was still young, popular and rich as Croesus. Now that he had inherited Halton, why should he not build something really splendid, with the amenities to entertain more spaciously (and perhaps less discreetly) than was possible in London? Such a grand design would give limitless pleasure to others, besides ensuring him the coveted status of country gentleman which his relatives found so agreeable.

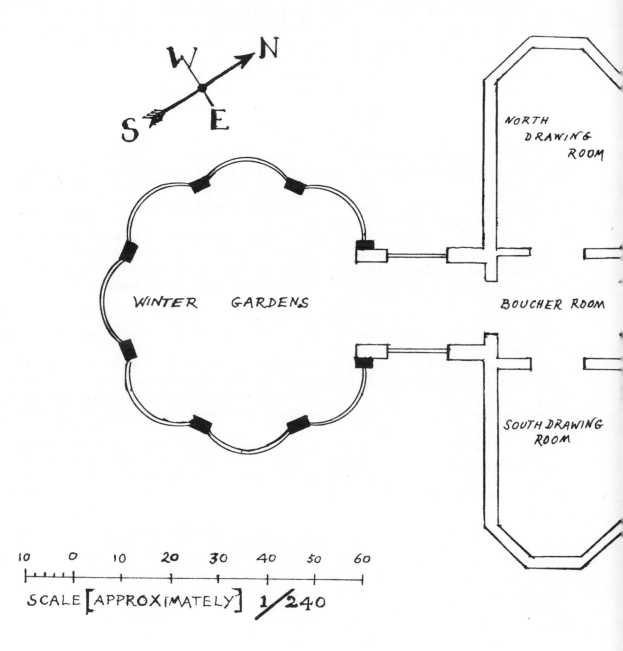

Thus the future of Halton for the next generation was determined: a grand new house and an estate redesigned for pleasure — and weekend pleasure at that. For this was to be no home in the conventional sense. It was to be — in the parlance of a later year — the plushest weekend bachelor pad in the country.

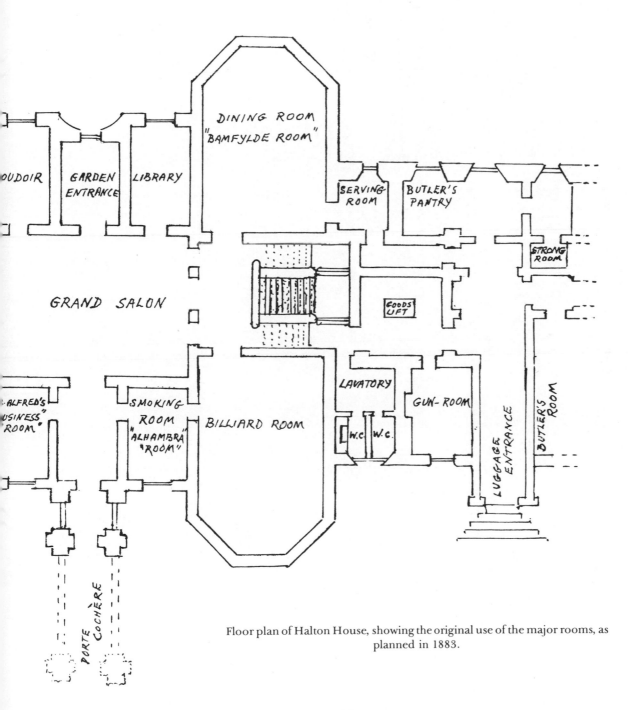

Floor plan of Halton House, showing the original use of the major rooms, as planned in 1883.

ABOVE: Halton House nearing completion in 1883; the architect is seated
at the centre first floor window; (HH) BELOW: Victorian foreman and
labourers in the foundations of Halton House. (Note the white glazed tile
bricks and lashed timber scaffolding.) (HP)

The Dome Decreed

'In Xanadu did Kubla Khan
A stately pleasure dome decree'
— *Samuel Taylor Coleridge*

The building of Halton Mansion started in 1881 and was completed in July 1883. (Before 1918 it was known as Halton Mansion [in contrast with the Dashwoods' Halton Manor] and the estate as Halton Park. Since 1918 it has been called Halton House). To comprehend Alfred's remarkable creation one has to put it in the context of that period.

The 1870s and 1880s saw a profound shift in the balance of the upper classes. Though the Rothschilds themselves had been established for over half a century, the floodgates were only just opening for most Victorian self-made millionaires. Iron masters, manufacturing tycoons, shipping magnates, railway barons and banking moguls — including many Jewish families — were at last breaking through the upper crust of society.

The Prince of Wales enjoyed the company of self-made men and, being constantly short of funds, needed them in a practical way; at Marlborough House he did more than anyone to encourage them socially, and the pages of Debrett and Burke opened reluctantly to admit them. In the country they gave sharp impetus to country house building which, as Girouard pointed out, reached its apogee in the 1870s.

These were, of course, trends which landed and mercantile aristocracy deplored, but the *nouveaux riches* did not care. Their wealth bought them the status they craved and they were not overawed by tradition. As a class they rejected the concept of English architecture propounded by Robert Kerr in his book *The Gentleman's House, or How to Plan English Residences from the Parsonage to the Palace.* It stated that a gentleman's home should be substantial but not showy, comfortable but not luxurious, a dignified vessel for Victorian family life and the modest entertainment of friends.

On the contrary they looked around for something which would shout to the heavens that they had more money and flair than any booby son of a duke or belted earl. And there was newly arrived in London the very thing, a dashing French Renaissance style direct from the Third Empire of Louis Napoleon, touched up here and there with overtones of Italianate and Byzantine — noone was too certain or too bothered.

It started appropriately enough with the London boom in hotel building in the 1860s. Huge commercial edifices sprang up in the new style, dominating central London's skyline: the Grosvenor Hotel, the Westminster Palace Hotel, the Charing Cross and the Langham with 'layer upon layer of rumbustious cornices and ornate windows, surmounted by bulbous roofs'. They were as flamboyant inside as out and the *nouveaux riches* adored every curlicue and whirligig.

This Renaissance reached its zenith in Baron Ferdinand's magnificent manor at Waddesdon, which was seven years in the making (1873-81). It was a mammoth undertaking, because

Ferdinand insisted on conquering a splendid and totally inaccessible site. A whole hill had to be levelled, 14 miles of railway track laid to convey hundreds of tons of Bath stone, and the water supply brought in sixteen miles from the Chilterns. Huge full grown elms and oaks were uprooted, hauled by teams of sixteen horses and replanted to satisfy the impatient demands of the owner. By the time Ferdinand was through (according to J.K. Fowler) he had spent over two million pounds on the house.

However, during these labours the fickle wind of fashion was already changing. Marc Girouard attributes this largely to the fate of Sir Albert Grant, a shady city financier who crashed in 1879. His own French Renaissance extravaganza stood half-built on a Kensington site for three years until it was demolished. The downfall of the Third Empire and the new Anglo-French colonial rivalry may have counted for something too.

In the event, Halton was the last fling of this bizarre architectural epoch and there was nothing half measured in its un-Englishness. Sir Nikolaus Pevsner bracketed it with Waddesdon rather backhandedly: 'When it comes to self assertiveness and an intrepid mixing of sources . . ., there is nothing in England to beat Waddesdon and Halton.' Interestingly Jill Franklin noted that the French Renaissance style was free of the Christian associations of Gothic, 'which probably explained one reason for its adoption at the Rothschild houses of Waddesdon and Halton'.

Comparisons between the two houses, which face each other some ten miles across the Vale of Aylesbury, come naturally; so too do comparisons between their owners, Alfred and Ferdinand, who were cousins. Both were passionate patrons of the arts who spent their lifetime amassing huge collections; both were leading society figures. Both were single men, for Alfred was a life-long bachelor and Ferdinand's bride, Alfred's sister Evelina, died in childbirth 18 months after their wedding in 1865. Both were fascinated by the French tradition in art and architecture. They were then natural rivals and perhaps in building his chateau Alfred was trying to upstage Ferdinand's own creation. Countess Warwick wrote of Halton: 'It was here that I saw Baron Ferdinand de Rothschild at a disadvantage for the only time in my life'. He was critical of the chateau and apparently jealous that Alfred's style of hospitality would outshine his own.

The similarities between the two houses, however, soon peters out. For Ferdinand chose a distinguished French architect, who rejoiced in the name of Hippolyte Alexandre Gabriel Walter Destailleur, to incorporate features of four classic *grands chateaux* into his massive Renaissance replica, and a French landscape gardener to lay out the grounds.

Alfred, on the other hand, commissioned the very English firm of William Cubitt and Company to execute the whole contract. The result was a composite 18th century dream chateau, less ponderous and even joyous by comparison.

The identity of the architect escaped earlier writers but survives in a massive Moroccan-bound photograph album preserved at Halton House with the inscription: 'To William R. Rogers, with sincere gratitude from Alfred de Rothschild, 1888'. A covering letter confirms that Rogers (or Rodriguez — his origins are obscure), who was the design partner of Cubbits, did the job.

William Cubitt and Co was the creation of the famous Cubitt brothers, Thomas (1788-1855) who *inter alia* built Osborne House for the Royal family and virtually invented speculative building, William (1791-1863), and the lesser-known Lewis. Separately and together they had established a nationwide practice in country houses and a reputation for sticking to a fixed price contract. After William's retirement in 1851 the firm was carried on by various partners.

Interestingly, between 1871-4 Cubitt's were building a large French Renaissance-style mansion at Wykehurst Park near Slaugham in Sussex, which incorporated cavity wall construction, fireproof floors, a lift, warm-air heating and other innovations. The owner was Henry Huth, son of a City finance house, and it is possible that Alfred may have visited him there. He would also have been impressed by 5 Hamilton Place, a luxurious town house which William Rogers had designed for his brother Leopold.

Halton Mansion was Cubitt's last independent contract. The firm was taken over in 1883, the year that Halton was finished, by Holland and Hannen. This would seem too close for coincidence, but whether the older firm overreached itself or achieved a reputation which made it an irresistible target is not clear.

A photograph taken on the Halton site in 1882-3 vividly illustrates the huge manpower demands of a major Victorian building project, before the advent of cranes, diggers and mechanical handling. Some 120 workmen are seen busy on a variety of tasks — roofing, glazing, bricklaying and landscaping — and they were only a small part of the labour force.

As 1883 drew on, the imposing north aspect of the Mansion rose above the unformed gardens, its stonework as white and pristine as the chalk slopes beneath. The huge bay windows and centre section rose gracefully on columns in two orders to the steep French pavilion roofs, which broke out into a galaxy of pinnacles and ornate chimney stacks. (They were soon to be joined by some thirty lightning conductors). In the centre a little round belfry was sited, its structure and approaches sheathed in a king's ransom in lead sheet.

The effect was theatrical and pleasing, the more so with a display of flags flying gaily from the roof.

The north side led directly onto a wide terrace and fine views over the Vale of Aylesbury. The south side was more or less identical, but with a deep *porte-cochère* as at Waddesdon, for carriages to pull out of the weather to allow the gentry to alight in comfort.

The Winter Gardens, at the west end, were the last stage to be completed. With two large domes and seven satellite domes the Gardens were to be a spectacular feature of the house.

In summer 1883 the structural work was complete: the builders moved out and an army of carpet layers, picture hangers and (a new type of workman) the electricians moved in.

Halton Mansion was the first house in the country to be *built*, rather than converted, for electrical lighting. Smallwood Manor in Staffordshire (completed in 1886) was quoted by Girouard as the first documented example that he was able to find. Halton's earlier claim is firmly based on a newspaper report of the gala opening in January 1884: 'The various apartments have been lit by electric light, softened down in incandescent lamps to a state in which many people thought it never could be brought when Mr. Edison first gave results of his researches in lighting to the astonished world'. The work was probably done by the forgotten firm of E.T. Mackrill in Aylesbury, who also fitted Alfred's coach for electricity. Mains supply was still years away and the power was provided by a generator in the old engine house in Halton village.

The central heating was another novelty, though not the first in the neighbourhood; at Mentmore Mayer had installed an early hot water system in the 1850s. Alfred's system was — and still is — a hot air system, whose workings remain largely inscrutable. Basically it is a hypocaust with water radiators the size of double beds sited in the basement under the floors of the great rooms. From them, square sectioned hot air flues run to grilles at floor level above. Like most Victorian systems it only warmed the major ground floor rooms and supplemented the Mansion's fourscore fireplaces. In consequence coal cellars the size of an underground car park were needed.

By mid-1883 another sort of housewarming was under discussion. A mansion of such magnificence needed an appropriate debut into society, something to make a splash. Alfred's opportunity came in July 1883 when the Prince of Wales was staying with Ferdinand at Waddesdon. He rode over to see his old Cambridge friend and view the new marvel. Being well acquainted with Alfred's lavish hospitality in London, HRH was graciously pleased to accept the invitation to be guest of honour at the forthcoming housewarming. Higher than that no host could aspire.

The great day was Saturday 19 January 1884. The Prince of Wales arrived by Royal train to Tring, to be met by Alfred in an open carriage. Tring, the *Buckinghamshire Herald* reporter remarked grudgingly, 'for once looked very gay'. A sour note came from Mr Chapman, superintendent of Herts Constabulary, who reported that 'not a few of the light fingered gentry were about'. A subscription had been floated to decorate the streets; all the shop fronts were decorated and illuminated, triumphal arches and illuminated loyal mottoes spanned the narrow High Street and Venetian masts fluttered in the cold night air.

It took an hour for the cavalcade to reach Halton, along a route lined by men and boys with torches and Chinese lanterns. At the Mansion the cream of Alfred's circle had been arriving all day, including the Prince of Saxe Coburg-Gotha, the Duchess of Manchester and a host of peers, baronets and society folk.

Dinner was served with the curtains open onto the gardens, which were floodlit by 12 huge arc lamps with parabolic reflectors installed on the roof. Their beams lit up both the Mansion — which was visible for miles around — and the statues in the gardens. Below the terrace, against the backdrop of young evergreens, the great fountain sent coloured plumes of water (illuminated by concealed lights) soaring skywards to represent the Prince of Wales' own emblem — the plume of feathers. It was much appreciated by the Prince, an old hand at such patriotic gestures, 'whose eyes so often rest upon sights and scenes of dazzling brilliance'.

The following day there was a large shooting party. Although fog prevented an early start, there was a reasonable bag of 200 brace. HRH did well, though the contemporary report tactfully omitted to say exactly how well.

The celebrations culminated in a grand ball. Carriages streamed up the drives to the illuminated chateau and the pick of Buckinghamshire society, the ladies in tiaras and white tulle court dresses, flocked to be presented to the Prince and to marvel at the chateau. For those who had been in any doubt, one thing was now quite clear. Alfred de Rothschild had arrived, and for the next thirty five years nothing in this corner of Buckinghamshire would ever be quite the same again.

A typical Rothschild frieze at Halton House, continuously repeated with lions, unicorns, family arrows and (elsewhere) AR monograms. (AA)

ABOVE: An unusual view of Tring High Street at the turn of the century, (AK) and BELOW: the newly completed chateau from the south aspect. Many of the shrubs and trees seen were planted nearly fully grown, to speed up the maturation of the gardens and grounds. (HH)

ABOVE: A slightly later view, showing the demarcation of the gardens from the parklands; the shepherd is Mr Charles Stevens; (HP) BELOW: 'Exaggerated nightmare' or 'imposing edifice . . . of classic grace and modern elegance'? The north aspect of Halton House at the height of its splendour, c1900. (HH)

'A Sumpshous Spot'

'It was a sumpshous spot all done up with gold with plenty of looking glasses'
— *Daisy Ashford* (The Young Visiters)

Unhappily not all of his contemporaries approved of what Alfred de Rothschild had done in this leafy corner of olde Englande.

Every description of Halton Mansion has included two thundering contemporary condemnations, as if they indicated universal opprobrium. Cecil Roth's *The Magnificent Rothschilds* (1938) started it, and subsequent authors found his quotations irresistible.

They are indeed intriguingly vitriolic. Algernon West described the Mansion in 1892 as 'an exaggerated nightmare of gorgeousness and senseless and ill applied magnificence'. (He added as an afterthought 'but lovely pictures'.)

Lady Frances Balfour, who walked over from Lady Rothschild's houseparty to view the newly completed chateau was appalled: 'I have seldom seen anything more terribly vulgar', she wrote; 'outside it is a combination of a French chateau and a gambling house. Inside it is badly planned and gaudily decorated . . . Oh, but the hideousness of the thing, the showiness! the sense of lavish wealth, thrust up your nose! . . . Eye hath not seen nor pen can write the ghastly coarseness of the sight'.

Such stuff, to be sure, is damning, until one enquires about these critics' credentials. (No-one previously has).

Sir Algernon West GCB was a public figure, and private secretary to William Gladstone. From 1881 to 1892 he was also Chairman of the Inland Revenue Board and perhaps the one man above all in England bound to condemn immoderate spending! As it was he came back again in 1895 and virtually recanted: 'On Christmas day, curiously enough, we dined at Alfred Rothschild's huge palace, Halton, which when lighted up and full of well dressed people, appeared quite tolerable'. For a tax man, that represents a fairly generous apology.

Lady Frances Balfour's background is even starchier. She was a true aristocrat, the daughter of the Duke of Argyll. Her husband was a brother of A.J. Balfour (Prime Minister in 1902-5), grandson of the Marquess of Salisbury, and latterly ADC to Edward VII. (Starch, in fact, does not come stiffer).

Though styled as Colonel (of the London Scottish Royal Volunteers) Balfour was a professional architect, FRIBA and FSA. He rebuilt much of Belgravia and Mayfair for the Duke of Westminster and represented the traditional school which despised the French vogue. To look for the blessing of the Balfours on Halton would be like asking the Spanish Inquisitors to bless the heretics.

Nor in considering contemporary opinions of Halton should one disregard the antisemitism of the period. As Countess Warwick wrote fifty years later: 'We resented the introduction of the Jews into the social set of the Prince of Wales; not because we disliked them individually . . . but because they had brains and understood finance. As a class, we did not like brains. As for money, our only understanding of it lay in the spending, not in the making of it'.

In fact most contemporary accounts found 'Mr. Alfred's Mansion at Halton' rather pleasing. True, an 18th century chateau in the Chilterns *was* incongruous, but some people liked that sort of thing. *Country Life* wrote of 'a great and imposing edifice, embodying in its architecture the pleasing characteristics of classic grace and modern elegance', and the local press of its palatial quality and faultless grounds. John Fowler eulogised 'a lovely mansion . . . not too large and replete with every elegance and luxury' while Alfred's cousin Constance Battersea gushed about his 'beauteous home on earth'. *The Architect* published photoengravings and the Mansion enjoyed great popularity with picture postcard companies. On the other hand, a minority found it downright nauseous (and some still do).

In drawing a balance between these views, the validity of one of Lady Balfour's objections has to be admitted. That is, the style in which Halton Mansion was built is not so much impure as promiscuous. It is as though designer William Rogers, having decided on the French interior and high pitched French pavilion roofs (a device to add height without extra masonry) then lost his nerve or confused the plans with another job. The lower parts of the house contain traces of Gothic, elements of the four classic orders, friezes of lions, unicorns, Austrian Eagles and Rothschild arrows which defy ascription, and even a sprinkling of the motifs of freemasonry. Architecturally it might be described as a Macedonian salad.

What of Lady Balfour's other main charge, that of vulgarity and 'ghastly coarseness'? This relates largely to the contemporary appearance and furnishings of the house at the end of the century. To judge them, fortunately we have a number of excellent primary sources which indicate how the main rooms were appointed and used. They include the architect's original plans, a fine set of photo plates commissioned by Alfred from Messrs Bedford Lemère in the 1880s and 1890s, several detailed first-hand accounts and Alfred's will, dated September 1917.

The basic plan of Halton was a rectangular house, whose ground floor consisted of four state rooms of identical dimensions, radiating from a lofty hall and linked by suites of smaller apartments. Then, as now, the focus of the interior is the central hall or salon, which rises through two storeys to a great glass dome, hung with massive chandeliers and set about with magnificent mirrors.

Entering through the main entrance, one's first impression of the chateau is of space — a room of some 65,000 cubic feet is unusual by any private standards. It is heightened by the magnificent split staircase ascending between bronze balustrades from the eastern end to the first floor balcony.

The second impression is of glittering gold. Nearly 40 years ago a young wartime RAF officer described it with poetic hyperbole: 'Merciful heaven! did anyone ever see so much gilt? It adorns every panel and every door, it wreathes itself into fantastic patterns and sackbut and shawms and other musical instruments, it overflows into baskets of flowers and horns of plenty. Here it is a quiver of arrows, there it is a sprightly nymph; it runs madly along the balcony that encircles the great hall and coruscates in the railings underneath; it twines demurely in loveknots, it runs amok in palanquins and tassels, or twirls itself frivolously into monograms . . . There is nothing shy or retiring or modest about it. It shouts at you like the sons of God and a good deal louder'. (Alfred's passion for AR monograms extended to almost all his possessions including some of the toilet seats.)

In the Rothschild period the white and gilt decor of the salon was contrasted with blue and gold Japanese curtains in the balcony arches, French silk tapestries by Neilson on the staircase and walls downstairs, gigantic antique Chinese vases, nude sculptures and much ornate French furniture. To the modern eye the contemporary photos of the salon convey an oppressive *embarras des richesses.*

The four great rooms off the salon form the corners of the main block. Each is over forty feet long, with spacious walls, high ceilings and large bay windows. The drawing rooms were Alfred's principal picture galleries, and their dimensions and lighting were designed for the best effects. The decor here was a mixture of Louis XV and XVI with fine wall tapestries. Leyland praised the overall effect, executed 'with such an artistic hand that carving, inlay, wall decoration and ceiling all conduce to a harmonious whole'.

The paintings were superb. Alfred built a magnificent collection of the 18th century French, Dutch and English schools to embellish Halton.

The South Drawing Room in its heyday was a profusion of rich red and green silks and the inescapable gilt, in which the ceilings, chairs and even the tables were picked out. The ceiling motifs are of delicate pastoral subjects involving tambourines, pipes and violas. In this room hung paintings by Lancret, Pater, Watteau and Teniers and a portrait of the famous French actress *Mademoiselle Dutet* by Drouais. It must have provided a stunning background for Alfred's musical soirées.

Between the South Drawing Room and the entrance vestibule lay the Business Room, though it is questionable if any business of a serious nature was ever transacted here. To the right of the fireplace hung Romney's portrait of Lady Hamilton dressed as Circe, painted about 1782. It was one of the finest of at least two dozen portraits Romney painted of his 'divine lady', and fetched £3,850 when sold at Christies in 1890. The scandalous young woman was an appropriate adornment for a bachelor's study.

The room contained two other Romneys, flower paintings by Van Heysum and a landscape by Hobbema. It also had as large a share of rococo as any other room in the house: the same gilt, opulent ceramics, heavy clocks, chandeliers and an ornate inlaid table. Even the wastepaper basket was gilded and velvet covered! This tends to disprove Roth's suggestion that because Alfred's own bedroom was small and simple, all the excesses of his homes much have been the fault of his advisers.

Between the South and North Drawing Rooms lay a vestibule called the Boucher Room. It contained four beautiful Bouchers illustrating various escapades by Venus. From it a stone vestibule of colonnades and shell shaped niches opened into the Winter Gardens. The gardens were heated and arranged with exotic flowers, mossy banks and palm trees which brushed the glass cupolas. A fine sculpture, Canova's *Dancing Girl* was positioned so that it was visible the length of the chateau from the main staircase.

The North Drawing room was sumptuous though less elaborate than the south-facing room, and it contained a score of masterpieces. There was a river scene by Albert Cuyp, two Bouchers, two Paters entitled *Peace* and *War,* two Lancrets and a dozen assorted masterpieces by Watteau, Wouvermans, Terburg and Greuze.

Next to the North Drawing Room in Alfred's day were two rooms which today are one — the Boudoir and the garden entrance. The Boudoir was a ladies' retiring room and thoroughly feminine with delicate filigree gilt on the ceiling. Gainsborough's portrait of *Mrs. Thicknesse* painted at Bath hung above an upright Sevres cabinet. Facing it was an antique mantlepiece which had once adorned the Petit Trianon and into which Wedgwood panels had been inserted.

Also on the north side and opening onto the terrace was the Dining Room, known in Alfred's time as the Bamfylde Room, since it was dominated by Joshua Reynolds' full length portrait of *Mrs. Bamfylde*, sometimes spelled *Bampfylde*. This picture is now in the Tate Gallery. Alfred had a copy painted for Lord Kitchener of Khartoum which was almost indistinguishable from the original.

Bedford Lemère photographed the room, which was elegantly panelled in white and gilt, during mid-week, with a modest table covered in white damask and laid for four. During a house party the room could comfortably hold twenty-five.

Opening off the Bamfylde room was what passed for Alfred's library. Bedford Lemere's photograph proves that the little dandy was no man of letters. Even his fond cousin, Lady Constance Battersea (the unlikely name was selected by her ennobled husband for political reasons) admitted of Alfred: 'He was no great reader, but had the art of picking the brains of other men and in this way acquired a great deal of information concerning many subjects'. In this highly literary age the bookcases seem pathetically small, obviously to avoid encroaching on the paintings. The room was dominated by landscapes and Dutch scenes. These included Teniers' *Card Party* and another painting depicting an *Interior of a Picture Gallery,*, in which he cunningly imitated in miniature his Dutch rivals while also painting likenesses of his father and himself. The cabinet contains some fine goldsmiths' work. (Alfred's outstanding specimen was the Pichon enamelled Orpheus cup in gold, now in the British Museum). On the mantlepiece is a set of five Sèvres vases in *bleu du roi,* embellished with medallion paintings.

So much for the frills. What volumes did Alfred deign to keep in his unconventional library? A hand lens over the original photoprint provides the answer: every identifiable title is a fine arts catalogue of some kind.

If Alfred was no citizen of the republic of letters he knew all about the Victorian tradition of billiards, which had come a long way since Byron and Lady Frances Webster started up an affair across a billiards table in 1813.

By 1880 billiards were as socially *de rigueur* for the gentlemen as pheasant shooting. Alfred's billiards room was on the south side of the salon opposite the Bamfylde room. Bedford Lemère's photograph shows it to good effect, lavishly panelled in gilded oak with an intricate gilded ceiling.

Around the massive carved table chesterfields were raised on a dais for a better view of the play. Here beneath a huge 17th century Dutch masterpiece by Jacob Jordaens, the gentlemen challenged each other and (as West recalled) pitted their skills against professional sharpsters and coaches whom Alfred brought down from London.

Leading from this elegant chamber, and connecting with the entrance vestibule where hung another Snyders masterpiece, *The Boar Hunt,* was the Smoking Room. After 1860 the incorporation of a smoking room or *tabagie* in a gentleman's home was considered obligatory. Usually it was built in tandem with the billiards room, but some houses incorporated smoking towers. (Cardiff Castle had two *tabagies,* for summer and winter use, in a tower 130 ft high).

Today Alfred's smoker — even though toned down — is of overpowering design. It has a gilded ceiling of such elaborate carving and coffering that the whole thing seems to be solid gold; it was estimated to have cost £25,000 in the 1880s. At that time the whole decor was extravagantly Moorish, and was known as the Alhambra Room. Oriental silks filled arabesque panels, Persian rugs covered the floor and the room reeked of the Turkish cigarettes and guinea cigars. Here the gentlemen relaxed away from the ladies — their irrepressible host donning a Turkish fez for the occasion — and swapped risque anecdotes and political confidences.

The rest of the house need not detain us long. The first floor contained grand bedroom suites and single rooms, all opening off the balcony. On the floor above them (and conversely lower on the social scale) were further guest rooms, smaller and with excellent views. At the top of the house, under the amazing roof, was a warren of servants' quarters, low-ceilinged and dark. Their existence cannot be suspected by anyone inspecting the building from the grounds, since Alfred did not care to have his servants overlook him at play. All the windows accordingly face inwards.

A socially intermediate position between the smaller guest rooms and the attic was occupied by the so called Chinese landing. Here the visitors of the lowest standing (entertainers, for example) were accommodated in rooms overlooking the service wing and sharing the kitchen noises.

What of life below stairs? As might be expected from his fastidious nature Alfred provided facilities for his servants which were Utopian compared with many Victorian households. The kitchen area was palatial, hygienically tiled in white glaze with separate bakery, sculleries, still room, silver room, huge store rooms, a game room and vast wine cellars and a beer cellar. 'All the usual offices' in a Rothschild house included separate rooms for the butler, housekeeper, maids, cooks, as well as a spacious servants' hall. It was all part of the plan to provide impeccable cuisine and service for guests.

There was also a lift, but not for personal transport, for no genteel person would travel in such a contraption. It took the tons of coal and luggage which had to be conveyed above stairs each weekend.

The household staff numbered over thirty and, from a surviving photograph, they looked satisfied enough. To wear the Rothschild badge was to these people, if not an honour, at least prestigious and exciting employment.

Exciting? Well, if the compensations of Victorian domestic service lay (as television writers would have us believe) in social glitter reflected from their employers, then the staff at Halton Mansion were indeed well rewarded.

The Grand Salon, a lushly appointed room of 65,000 cubic feet, rising through two storeys to a great glass dome. (HH)

41

ABOVE: The South Drawing Room, where great opera singers like Melba and Patti sang for a charming 'little gift' (worth twice their top fee) from their host; (HH) LEFT: the classic lines of the Winter Gardens, where palms and orchids flourished. The statue is Canova's *Dancing Girl*, (HH) and RIGHT: view of the Winter Gardens through 'Marble Arch' and into the Grand Salon; Alfred's private orchestra played frequently here. (KD)

ABOVE: The sumptuous North Drawing Room, c1894; (NMR) LEFT: the Boudoir (or ladies' retiring room) off the north side of the Salon. Gainsborough's portrait of *Mrs Thicknesse* hangs above three Sèvres vases, (HH) and RIGHT: the Bamfylde Room, named after Joshua Reynold's portrait of *Mrs Bamfylde,* seen here. The room was photographed at midweek with the banqueting table cleared away. (NMR)

OPPOSITE ABOVE: The Bamfylde Room, laid for guests, thought to be during the visit of the Shah of Persia in 1897, (BC) and BELOW: 'He was no great reader'; a view of Alfred's library, in which the paintings were afforded far more space than the books; (NMR) ABOVE: 'Mr Alfred's Business Room'; Romney's portrait of *Lady Hamilton* hangs beside the fireplace. (HH)

ABOVE: The Billiards Room, panelled in gilded oak; the billiards table is still in daily use by members of the Officers' mess at Halton; (HH) BELOW: 'Upstairs, downstairs' — group photo of Alfred's kitchen staff. (BC)

The great double-return staircase, pictured in the 1890s: the Rothschild motif of five arrows and Alfred's monogram (AR) recur frequently on the balustrade. (RAFH)

ABOVE: The Alhambra Room, Alfred's very Moorish smoking room; its lavish ceiling is reputed to have cost £25,000, even in 1883! (RAFH) and BELOW: some of Alfred's domestic servants pose on the steps of the luggage entrance. (HP)

ABOVE: Liveried manservants at Halton; at far right on the back row is
Trodd, the butler; (BC) BELOW: the kitchens at Halton House — the Italian
sous-chef is giving the pastry cook a particularly admiring look. (BC)

49

ABOVE: Velvet lawns and sweeping drives; the south aspect of the chateau in the 1890s; (NMR) LEFT: 'They were so lovely and small . . .'; a rare picture of one of Alfred's circus ponies, complete with bells but not electric lights, (KD) and RIGHT: one of the Halton footmen puts a circus pony through its paces. (HP)

Weekend in the Country

'From Halton we brought with us the impression that we had been wafted for a spell to Fairy land and were dwelling in a place of Enchantment.' — *Mrs Clement Scott*, Old Days in Bohemian London

Alfred Rothschild's concept of hospitality was simple: nothing was too extravagant, too showy or too much trouble (for the servants) so long as everyone was having a thoroughly good time.

At Halton Mansion he elevated the Victorian weekend house party from what Disraeli called 'the monotony of organized platitude' into a cult of novelty and sensuousness.

The indulgence started with the journey down from London — by private train specially reserved by the host. At Tring Station (or after 1892 at Wendover) the guests were met by a carriage, magnificent in the Rothschild livery of dark blue and yellow tracing, and in later years by an automobile with the carriage discreetly parked behind. The former represented Alfred's pioneering spirit and the second his sense of caution.

Through the dusty streets of Tring they went, up the Icknield Way between pastures of fat sheep and into beechwoods. Along the route was a welcoming party of estate servants, wearing blue and yellow Rothschild scarves (and fleece lined greatcoats in winter), stationed at every corner. Each man held red and white flags and a lantern after dusk — another of Alfred's precautions against motoring mishaps.

As the party arrived, the evening sun was shining on the white exterior of the chateau, on peacocks strutting on velvet lawns, on sweeping drives and innumerable flower borders. Outside on the steps or by the stone and metal structure that is still curiously reminiscent of Eros, was their host, dapper and fresh — thanks to his enlightened custom of not working on Fridays.

The guests were as brilliant as the setting: not as politically imposing as Nattie's parties at Tring, where the young Winston Churchill made contacts to advance his career, nor so horsey as Leopold's at Ascott and certainly not as intellectual as Aunt Louise's literary circle at Aston Clinton, which included Macaulay, Tennyson, Browning and Matthew Arnold. They were a blend of the richest, the wittiest and the most talented that the *fin de siècle* offered: blue bloods, ambassadors, millionaire bankers, society beauties like Lily Langtry, Gertie Miller and the Prince of Wales' favourite Daisy Pless, soldiers like Lord Kitchener, politicians of every rank and hue, Harley Street doyens like Sir Milsom Rees, art connoisseurs like Sir Joseph Duveen and Sir Guy Laking and wits like Lord Charles Beresford. (Beresford was reputedly the wittiest man in England. Only he could have got away with the famous telegram declining a weekend invitation from the Prince of Wales: 'Can't possibly. Lie follows by post'.)

If there were a 19th century equivalent of today's 'beautiful people', they were among those who signed the guest book at Halton Mansion.

Often the parties were as cosmopolitan as Alfred himself. When Sir Algernon West dined there in December 1895, eight nationalities were represented at table, including an Indian prince, the

Brazilian ambassador, the Belgian ambassador and the Marquis de Soveral, who was first attaché at the Portuguese embassy and a bosom friend of Alfred. (Known as the Blue Monkey because of his swarthy chops, he was a famous ladykiller and subsequently President of Portugal). Another intimate was Baron von Eckardstein, secretary to the German Embassy.

No matter what their station, there were few who did not gasp as they were ushered into the chateau for the first time, ablaze with new-fangled electrical lights and perfumed by arrays of flowers from Alfred's hot houses. The colours of the tapestried walls and furnishings blended breathtakingly with the richness of the paintings.

When the company repaired to their rooms to dress, they found baskets filled with huge sprays of flowers from which to select their corsages or boutonnières for dinner — another example of Alfred's flair.

Dinner was never served before nine o'clock. The reason was considered quaint but it was typical of Alfred: he insisted that the servants had their supper first! The delay was more than compensated for by the cuisine of a master chef and the finest *premiers crus* from the Mouton Rothschild vineyards. A speciality of the house was *poussin haltonais,* young out-of-season pheasants which had their necks wrung to circumvent the Game Laws. New delicacies from Europe were likely to be on Alfred's table before London society had tasted them.

It was the same with the conversation, for the network of Rothschild agents throughout Europe's capitals had orders to forward not only financial news to New Court, but whatever good anecdote or scandal was abroad. The Prince of Wales was particularly fond of Jewish jokes, which the three Rothschild brothers good-naturedly collected for him. So Alfred, toying with his food at the head of the table, was primed to lead conversation as effervescent as the champagne.

After dinner there was a choice of entertainment. How about a full orchestral concert? That was no problem, for Alfred maintained his own string orchestra at Halton, a luxury even by Rothschild standards. The musicians were selected not only for their skill but also for their comparable heights and identical moustaches. After dinner the master of Halton, never able to resist the limelight, would step up to conduct, with an ivory baton encrusted with diamonds. Two of his batons are still preserved by his family. (On one occasion, responding to a suggestion by Lady Constance Battersea, who was strong on Good Works, that he might do something for the inmates of Aylesbury Gaol, he sent the orchestra along to play for them. The players were astonished by their rapturous reception.)

Next, some of the guests would be invited to perform. This was no mean entertainment, for Alfred's parties included the world's greatest operatic stars. The South Drawing Room reverberated to the divine Melba (whose financial affairs he managed) and to another immortal soprano, Adelina Patti, together with her less distinguished husband Niccolini, the French tenor, and to Edouard de Reszke, the Polish bass. Alfred's influence with Patti was so strong that he alone could induce her to break a lifelong habit and perform at the Gala Night which he arranged at Covent Garden during the Boer War for the war charities. The prices were staggering: £250 for a box and £15 for a stall.

Among composers and pianists he counted Liszt (who died in 1886, before Halton was long established) and Rubinstein as friends; among violinists the Spanish virtuoso, Pablo Sarasate, the Belgian Eugene Ysaye and the Russian Mischa Elman, whom Alfred 'discovered'.

Such were the musical divinities who filled Alfred's great rooms with music, but never performed for anything so vulgar as a fee. Roth recounts how Alfred used to pride himself on the alacrity with which his *prima donnas* accepted the invitation to sing, and he would point out that they did it *gratis.* He avoided mentioning that the 'little gift' which he gave them at the end — usually an item of jewellery — was worth twice as much as the highest fee they could command.

For variety, or if musical virtuosos were lacking, there might be a conjuror, magician or ventriloquist brought over from the continent, or performing dogs, whose behaviour could be too capricious for comfort. They first appeared at the housewarming party before the Prince of Wales in 1884, and Lady Warwick noted: 'He exhibited a number of Japanese dogs which had been taught to perform. Great confusion was caused by the fact that, although the chief little dog performed, it was not according to the programme'.

Alfred's passion for gadgets led him to have a newly invented instrument called an orchestrion installed under the staircase. A guest described it as 'a combination of a barrel organ, a harmonium, a penny trumpet and Jew's harp, with poker and tongs knocked down at intervals' — a rather vulgar gimmick.

Later, if the mood took the company, there would be dancing far into the night. (When you happen to own the orchestra there are no restrictions on hours). Finally the guests would get to bed, senses and appetites sated. If they woke to heavy footsteps, as did Mrs Scott, it was only the nightwatchmen patrolling the corridors and guarding Alfred's treasures.

One variation of Alfred's brilliant evenings was what he called his 'adoration dinners'. These had a flavour of the Naughty Nineties and probably (for convenience) took place in London rather than the country. They were dinner parties to which three or four close male friends were invited, together with a particularly beautiful woman whom Alfred wished to impress. After the meal there was a little ritual where Alfred would take his lady guest to one side and whisper 'What shall I give you, beautiful lady?', and then present her with some charming curio which had been carefully selected beforehand.

On one occasion, Lily Langtry, who was a frequent star at these adoration occasions, nearly ruined the evening. When Alfred asked: 'And what shall I give you, beautiful lady?', she picked up a priceless enamelled and diamond-studded Louis XVI snuff box lying on a table and said carelessly: 'Oh, this will do'. Later she wrote: 'He had a weak heart and for a moment I thought I had stopped it. When he got his breath he promised me something much prettier and out came one of the well known gift boxes'. The story is reminiscent of another great artiste and intimate of Alfred Rothschild, Gertie Miller. She capped a theatrical career by marrying the Earl of Dudley. At the betrothal her intended sent round two engagement rings for her to select the better. She kept both.

The luxuries of a Rothschild house were no less by day than by night. As Prime Minister Asquith discovered, they started early in the morning with the curtain being drawn. He told the story of Waddesdon but, as Miss Cowles points out, it might as easily have been of Halton. A powdered footman was followed by an underling propelling a dumb waiter, set for all contingencies. After the guest had been gently wakened, the flunkey politely enquired:

'Tea, coffee or a peach off the wall, Sir?

'Tea please'.

'China tea, Indian tea, or Ceylon tea, Sir?'

'China, if you please'. But the litany continued:

'Lemon, milk or cream, Sir?'

'Milk please'.

'Jersey, Hereford or Shorthorn, Sir?'

Rarely can the British early morning tea ritual have been taken to greater lengths.

Later there was a choice of diversions. One could follow the Rothschild Staghounds, which frequently met at Halton Mansion, though Alfred himself was no great horseman. Or there might be a shoot for the gentlemen, to which the little dandy steeled himself because it was the done thing. He possessed some beautiful Purdy twelve-bores and a sizeable gun room at Halton, but he did not care for the sport. Who could forget the fate of poor Uncle Alphonse who, while organising a pheasant *battue* at Ferrières, was accidentally shot in the face by some idiotic guest and thereby lost an eye? Baron Alphonse was actually Alfred's second cousin, but he was also his brother-in-law, having married Lionel's elder daughter Leonora, a typical example of Rothschild consanguinity. Incidentally, the Baron, with admirable chivalry, never revealed the name of his mutilator.

Thus when Alfred and his guests took up their stands around the coverts, Alfred's gamekeepers had already been out for hours, plugging up the rabbit holes with cloths and cutting any brambles that might trip the gentlemen. They were followed at a discreet distance from the guns by Alfred's private doctor in a pony trap with all his medical gear, just in case.

Meanwhile the ladies promenaded in the gardens to admire the accomplishments of Alfred's sixty gardeners, the beautiful trees and shrubs collected from every corner of Europe, fantastic flowering cornucopiae, the shady walks, the secluded lawns and the Italian gardens. Down by the lake was an Indian tent, actually a permanent building with stout walls and a solid roof, where the servants prepared refreshments. They could stroll over to the hot houses in the village, where fruit and flowers of extraordinary richness were grown. The home farm was regarded as something of a marvel and was particularly strong on poultry.

Then there were all the outdoor diversions beloved of the later Victorians: lawn tennis, croquet, boating on the reservoirs, cricket matches on Alfred's own sports field with its handsome brick-built pavilion, champagne picnics on the lawns or transported into the Chiltern glades by uniformed footmen. There was even an indoor swimming pool — an innovation of which Mama would never have approved — naughtily hidden in the recesses of the basement. History does not relate whether the bathing was mixed or segregated.

A typical Alfredian touch — which prevented the whole week-end from becoming too routine — was his private circus. No lions or bears — nothing so barbaric, but ponies, birds and the little performing dogs with the unpredictable ways. They lived in a menagerie not far from the chateau, with a circus ring in the woods. The climax of a performance always came when Alfred stepped out, dressed in a blue frock coat, lavender kid gloves and a long whip, and took over as ringmaster. It was a symbolic moment, the little exhibitionist standing among sawdust and arc lights, cracking his whip to send the pets through the hoop, while his society friends applauded with a bemused and good natured sarcasm.

It was this exhibitionism in Alfred which made him a figure of ridicule — not so much the ostentation of his possessions, whether circus, orchestra or chateau. Small wonder that Max Beerbohm took such malicious delight in cartooning him. He made an enormous target.

This is to overlook the real pleasure his possessions afforded, and not just to his guests. Nearly seventy years later, the daughter of one of Alfred's estate workers remembered being taken to see the circus ponies: 'It was fairyland come true. They were so lovely and small and they were all cream coloured. Their harnesses and trappings were covered in coloured electric bulbs . . . and each little pony had its own head dress with its name in electric bulbs. I have often thought of them and wondered what happened to them when Mr Alfred died'.

One piece of showiness that has been wrongly credited to Alfred was the zebra-drawn carriages. Zebras were part of the magnificent natural history collection that was growing up at Tring Park, under the direction of Walter Rothschild, which would eventually become part of the British Museum. Walter had stuffed zebras in his museum and live zebras prancing with the emus and elk in the park; he even had a new species of zebra named after him. From time to time for the amusement of family and friends, the zebras were pressed into service, either to draw a single trap or a coach plus four, ie three zebras and a pony. The leading pony was essential because without it the team was unmanageable, which was no joke when it was being drawn down Pall Mall.

The style was pure Rothschild and Alfred may have wished he had thought of it himself. He may even have borrowed Walter's exotic team from time to time, but it was a Tring phenomenon, not a Halton one.

One great advantage of a weekend with Alfred was that it was free of the kill-joy religious observances of Gentile households. (Piety also afflicted weekends at Aston Clinton where, on the Saturday [Jewish Sabbath], the carriages were not allowed out and the ordinary household routines were suspended.) St Michael's Church at Halton was within sight of the chateau for guests who were unprepared to defy convention, and for the rest — well, there were so many enchanting things to be done and the weekend was not getting younger.

A trip to the chalet? — yes, that *was* an enchanting thing, just right for a Sunday afternoon. To give his Sunday outings an objective, Alfred decided not on a folly but on a real summer house in the woods. In 1888 he commissioned an Austrian architect to build an Austrian chalet in a superb position, surrounded by turfy meadows and pine trees on the crest of the Chiltern escarpment high above the Vale. It stands there still, a true chalet of wooden timbers on a brick foundation with a balcony running round the ground floor. All the timber came from the Halton woods.

This lonely and beautiful spot had been the unconventional burial ground of an 18th century rustic, a shepherd-philosopher named Faithful. Chamber's *Book of Days* (1863) recalls that for decades his epitaph could be seen cut into the chalk beneath the turf:

> 'Faithful lived and Faithful died,
> Faithful lies buried on the hillside.
> The hill so wide the fields surround,
> In the day of Judgement he'll be found.'

Before the chalet was built Alfred ordered the top of the hill levelled, and the earthworks brought to light the bones of Faithful and his dog. They were decently reinterred in a spot not far from the chalet.

To this place the house party would drive in open carriages, up the winding way between the beeches and pines. At the top they were rewarded, as John Leyland found, with spectacular views: 'The visitor is lost in admiration as he surveys the vast panorama — a country of exceeding richness, chosen long ago for the seats of noblemen and gentlemen'. In the wooded foreground are the pinnacles and parklands of Halton far below. The land stretches away over Buckinghamshire to the blue hills beyond Oxford in one direction, and in the other beyond Hertfordshire to the gentle greenness of South Bedfordshire.

At the chalet the caretaker and servants had already prepared a sumptuous tea on the balconies, and afterwards there was an indoor skittle alley and a crowd of spaniels with whom to play.

Alfred was so delighted with his new plaything that he brought the Prince of Wales to look over it. The conversation must have gone along these lines:

'Charming, my dear Alfred, charming. But a little bare, don't you think?'

'*Bare,* sire?'

'Yes, all that wooden boarding and knot holes. Needs some ivy climbing up over the balconies. Give it a bit of maturity, y'know.' A slight shudder from Alfred, whose fastidious tastes recoiled from ivy — untidy trailing stuff harbouring nasty insects! But *le prince veult,* and when Edward next came it was to find the balconies groaning under the festoons of ivy. Closer examination showed that the leaves and stalks were made in metal, attached to ironwork screens. Science had triumphed over nature, but nature finally got her own back. When the winds blew up from Aylesbury Vale the mass of metal pieces jangled in a *danse macabre* which nearly maddened the early RAF tenants of the chalet. The whole lot was consigned to the undergrowth in the 1920s.

Another success was the skating lake. One winter day late in the century, so the story goes, Alfred rang Halton from London. He was entertaining a youthful crowd from town that weekend and there was to be skating at Halton.

'Very good, Mr Alfred', replied Frederick Hubbard, the estate manager. (Surely the master did not intend taking to the *canal*?) But no, for there followed a list of instructions to dig and line a sizeable lake — in the space of a few days. It was the devil to complete in time, since the bitter weather prevented the mortar setting properly, but somehow it was done.

The great dish-shaped lake, 80 yards across, was a glorious feature of the old estate. The Indian tent was built beside it and in winter it presented that most delightful of Victorian scenes — ladies in muffs and ermine coats gliding gracefully, while the gentlemen in cut-away coats pirouetted and preened — or crashed to the ice. Meanwhile (on duty as always) Alfred's doctor took a hot toddy in the tent and prayed fervently that if anyone broke a leg it would not be Alfred.

In summer the lake became an ornamental pond and a focal point during Alfred's agricultural shows. Like the ivy, it did not survive the RAF's accession for long. It was still in use until the late '20s, when young officers would line their cars around the edge and skate by the headlight beams. Today the rink is overgrown and buried in a fir tree plantation.

By Sunday night the guests were surfeited, but they did not go away empty-handed. Boxes of orchids and other hot house blooms were produced for the ladies, and boxes of their host's famous guinea cigars for the gentlemen. (These became so well known that one manufacturer marketed an 'Alfred de Rothschild' cigar. The same had happened to Alfred's friend Edward de Reszke, who unwittingly christened a cigarette.) Great hampers of exotic fruit, cakes, and chocolates for the visitors' children were packed into each brougham or motor car.

It has been said with some justice that all this lavish spending might have been better diverted to charities and good works. But Alfred tended to leave that sort of thing to other members of the family. His own generosity was more personal; no friend appealed in vain, no servant went unrewarded, no reasonable request was ever ignored — even though his generosity often had little relation to the worthiness of the cause. There were significant sporadic exceptions: the London Hospitals (especially St Mary's), the Boer War appeals and Jewish good works. The residue of his estate was left with remarkable impartiality to be divided by his trustees among such Jewish and Christian charities as they thought fit.

The last word goes to Mrs Clements, the wife of the *Daily Telegraph* theatre critic: 'Mr Rothschild had money in plenty and to spare, but he knew how to spend it in helping to give other people happiness'.

Perhaps in an age when a tiny two-and-a-half per cent of the population owned two-thirds of the nation's wealth, when gambling, horse racing, and fast selfish living were the norm among the monied classes, it was not such a bad epitaph.

56

OPPOSITE: An open carriage, with beautifully groomed horse, waits on the north terrace at Halton House; (ES) ABOVE: Lionel Walter, second Lord Rothschild and Alfred's nephew, in one of the famous Tring zebra traps (RGG) and BELOW: the Austrian chalet in Halton woods, focus of many house-party excursions — original sketch by R. Sinclair. (KD)

ABOVE: A forgotten glory of old Halton: this ornamental lake-cum-winter skating rink today lies buried in a small plantation; (NMR) BELOW: the Halton game keepers, preparing to feed the pheasant poults. (HP)

ABOVE: Gamekeepers and beaters departing on a shoot; the timber-frame building, known as the Kennels, still stands in Halton village; (HP) BELOW: the estate carpenters, several of them holding the tools of their trade. (HP)

ABOVE: The Italian gardens, with a marble and mosaic terrace and ivy-trained alcoves containing classical statues; Italian workmen were reputedly brought over to create the scene; (RG) BELOW: view across a lily pond on the north west aspect; one of Alfred's Indian tents is extreme right. (SP)

A Squire for all Seasons

'O let us love our occupations,
Bless the squire and his relations,
Live upon our daily rations
And always know our proper stations'. — *Charles Dickens*

One of the most coveted goals of the Victorian *nouveau riche* was the status of the squire; the possession of broad acres and a county seat could put a stamp of respectability on a lifetime spent slitting throats in commerce.

Now the essence of squirearchy, as most of the Rothschilds appreciated, was physical residence; ignorance of this fact sent the French aristocracy to the guillotine. Gallivanting for a few weeks a year in London was quite in order, but one had to *live* in the country to identify thoroughly with the interests of tenants and neighbours.

There were those like Harry Chaplin, squire of Blankney in Lincolnshire and a friend of Alfred, who tried to get the best of both town *and* country. E. F. Benson wrote charmingly of him: 'He raced, he shot, he hunted, he warmed both hands at the numerous fires of life and with both he scattered money as if Pactolus flowed from the park at Blankney'. And in the end, between being both Champagne Charlie and country squire, he went broke and lost everything.

For Alfred Rothschild there was no such dilemma. The call of society and of foreign travel was too strong. Nevertheless he *was* a Rothschild and everything had to be done properly. That meant keeping up appearances on the estate, maintaining full employment and exercising that peculiar brand of Rothschildean paternalism. The difference was that in Alfred's case it was largely done by proxy.

The proxy was Frederick Hubbard, Alfred's agent at Halton. A large imposing figure with fashionable Edwardian beard and moustachioes, he was a tireless substitute, even though plagued by gout. (Like many of the servants he found his loyalty richly remembered in Alfred's will. Hubbard received £5,000 cash and his son Jack, his own right hand man, £500. Trodd the butler got £3,000.)

One way and another Alfred supported virtually the whole of Halton village, whose population of 200 had altered little in 100 years, and a fair part of Aston Clinton. His personal payroll — excluding tenant farmers and their men — was well over 100 souls.

Just where did this small army work? Between 30 and 40 were in domestic service; in addition no less than sixty were gardeners. Alfred had twelve sturdy estate carpenters growing old in his service, and a half dozen gamekeepers. On shoot days they were turned out in brown corduroy jackets and waistcoats with brass 'AR' buttons, twill breeches and bowlers.

Rather more remarkable was Alfred's personal fire brigade of twelve professionally equipped pompadours and a horse-drawn fire engine. They were not simply ornamental, for Alfred had a phobia of fire among his paintings at the chateau. The firemen, to the delight of the villagers, practised regularly in his absence and were invaluable for dowsing hayricks and rescuing cats. So far as is known they were never needed in earnest at the chateau. Perhaps this was just as well. When the Army Inspector General of Fire Services inspected the mansion in 1918 he found the pressure so low that the hydrants could not reach the upper storeys! But that may have been because the Army had diverted so much water.

In the earlier years the stables required a great deal of fresh labour as grooms, coachmen and stable boys. But, like his brother Leopold, Alfred soon went overboard for the motor car. He had a fine collection of early Buckinghamshire machines, including the 55th and 56th to be registered in the shire (December 1903). His most elegant specimens were a Rolls Royce and a 1 ton Renault.

The remaining employees were labourers on the home farm, foresters, lodge keepers, horsemen and mechanics.

Alfred may not have known them all by name, but he remembered their comforts. Halton was probably the only estate in England where a cart went round at midday with urns of hot coffee for all the workers, and again in the afternoon with sandwiches, cake and tea.

Of all these outdoor enterprises the gardens were the most fascinating. Sixty gardeners, men and boys, was a staggering number even for those days of cheap labour; a young Halton gardener in 1900 earned sixteen shillings a week.

Alfred, however, was an excessively demanding and impatient employer, who would have caused one strike a day in latter 20th century England. Ernest Field, who arrived as a journeyman propagator in 1900, recalled seventy years later: 'The first advice I was given was never say no to Mr. Rothschild. If he tells you to put a ladder to the moon, then you go off and get the ladder, at least'.

In the early years the main problem was carving gardens out of rough, centuries-old Chiltern pastures and urging them into instant maturity. This meant wherever possible planting trees and shrubs which were already half grown. An early picture, probably taken by the butler Trodd who was a keen photographer, shows sheep grazing almost up to the house. But smelly sheep were not Alfred's fancy. The landscaping forged ahead around the lawns on the northern slope. There were German *parterres,* replicas of the beds Alfred had fallen for when taking the waters near Hamburg; Italian gardens with a mosaic-tiled promenade between fragrant ivy bowers and rose beds leading to a little classical temple; fountains and water grottoes with water cascading between pools and nearby, in a shady grove, the Indian tent where the Shah of Persia enjoyed an *après déjeuner* cigarette. This was during the Shah's visit in July 1889. (He was taken on a whirlwind tour of Hatfield, Ashridge, Halton (where he stayed for lunch) and Waddesdon, before proceeding rather more seriously to do some shopping at the Birmingham Small Arms factory.) The walks and glades were all the more fascinating for Alfred's obsession with the exotic. Visitors were astonished at the tropical palms and mountain shrubs which had no business to be thriving there at all.

Thus by a coalition of limitless labour and money-no-object, Alfred's staff were able to do what he demanded of them. They accelerated nature and within a decade made the gardens — to quote numerous sources — look as if they had been established for generations.

Even then, there was no respite for the gardeners. The floral demands of the huge rooms at Halton and Seamore Place were endless; Alfred's schemes for table decorations of orchids, caladiums (of which Halton produced over 100 species) and other exotica were so complex that a specialist from Veitch's came down with wooden gauges, to check the height and width of each arrangement. The diminutive host was not going to have the dinner repartee spoiled by being unable to see his guests.

In Edwardian horticultural circles it used to be said that one could tell a man's status by the size of his bedding list, thus: 10,000 plants for a squire; 20,000 for a baronet; 30,000 for an earl; 50,000 for a duke.

By that tally Alfred aimed pretty high; his total in 1903 of 40,418 put him half way between an earldom and dukedom. Every year, working in 50 glass houses in the village which covered acres of glass, the gardeners struck no less than 10,000 carnations and potted almost as many lilies of the valley.

Alfred's own interventions did not help, since he had a sublime ignorance of the seasons. Field recalled how once he conceived a fancy to have one of the tall columns supporting the Winter Gardens decorated: 'Roses! Rambler roses all the way up! I'd like to see them next time I come'.

It was midseason and entirely the wrong time to be moving roses, but the gardeners' honour was at stake. Sanders the head gardener obtained a load of potted ramblers from Veitch's which reached halfway up the columns. They filled in the top sections with matching *artificial flowers* notched into green painted bamboos and kept their fingers crossed. The fakes would not have stood close inspection, but on his next visit Alfred merely remarked 'Lovely' and all was well.

On another occasion a long dry spell scorched the shallow rooted lawns and the chalk beneath began to show through. Indignant at the motheaten sight, Alfred threatened to have the slopes *painted* green. Fortunately for his long-suffering staff the weather changed, and it was never known if he was serious.

Even at Halton, however, there was more to life than work. During the golden Edwardian years when Alfred was gadding around less and enjoying the fruits of his servants' labours more, his generosity was as liberal as on any of the Rothschild estates.

To the children of Halton and surrounding villages he became an invisible Santa Claus with only the vaguest idea of the calendar. Christmas, Guy Fawkes, Alfred's birthday, Coronations, Jubilees, church fêtes, cricket matches — all were red letter days on which exciting treats suddenly materialised.

One such red letter day was the coronation festivities for Alfred's old friend Edward VII in June 1902. It may be remembered how Edward, taken seriously ill with appendicitis, had to postpone the ceremony. Nevertheless the King insisted that the countrywide festivities should continue.

Alfred complied, and on 26 June the entire populations of Halton, Wendover and Weston Turville flocked to Halton Park as his guests. A brass band and free drinks ('both excisable and otherwise') started the day in best Rothschild fashion. No less than 1,200 men and boys over 15 years sat down to a slap-up luncheon in a massive marquee, and each was later presented with a briar pipe and ounce of tobacco. In the afternoon the kids swarmed over the sideshows, while a hired repertory company entertained the adults with a newfangled comedy called *Charley's Aunt.* Then the men crowded back into the beer tents and the children and mothers enjoyed a sumptuous tea, followed by a performance of *Aladdin.* What with penny whistles, coronation mugs, Punch and Judy, swings and roundabouts, Dad half-sozzled in the beer tent and finally a Christmas panto, it was no wonder the childrens' concept of Mr Alfred was a bit hazy. Elderly inhabitants of Halton still remember his amazing Christmas liberality in disbursing a whole shilling to each village child.

They can hardly be blamed, for on this day — as on so many occasions — Alfred did not put in an appearance.

This was the curious pattern of Alfred's munificence among his people. Over the years acres of canvas were erected over feasts he never tasted, his health was toasted in seas of wines which he never touched and countless stanzas of *For He's a Jolly Good Fellow* were rousingly sung by the lower orders — but never heard.

For Mr Alfred was always away in town, in Scotland or abroad. He sometimes sent a seigneurial salutation to be read out by faithful Hubbard or by the Rector, but for the most part he simply wrote the cheques.

His bounty extended also to the City of London Police and Buckinghamshire Constabulary, who were regularly bidden to Halton Park for lavish cricket matches. Alfred adored being saluted by policemen, and this was a good means of encouraging them in their duty.

Nothing demonstrated his curious combination of generosity and disinterest better than the long succession of agricultural shows which were held at Halton Park before the First World War. It will be recalled that Halton was the site of a pioneer show in 1868 which was part-industrial and part-agricultural; a generation later, many villages and towns had followed suit. The new foreign competition in farming and the need for communication between farmers and suppliers gave agricultural shows some importance. There was keen discussion on crops, equipment and prices.

It was inevitable that the Rothschilds should participate in something so close to the soil. In the 1890s the Tring Agricultural Society show was transferred to Lord Rothschild's spacious parklands with gratifying results. At the same time the annual show of the Chiltern Hills Agricultural Association, approaching its 50th anniversary, was dying on its feet. In 1900 the Committee obtained Alfred's consent to use Clay Field on the Wendover side of Halton Park as the show site, and thereafter it never looked back.

Once involved (and of course elected President) Alfred backed the thing with the largesse of a major banking venture. Rothschild money and labour carried the show from strength to strength until, in 1913, with the day's gate at over 7,000, it was considered the best in the county.

Perhaps nothing is so redolent of the balmy Edwardian years as the newspaper reports of those summer shows. The sun (it seems) always shone brilliantly from cloudless skies on a happy rural scene; the ladies in wide flower hats and parasols, the gentlemen in boaters and blazers, red faced farmers in corduroys, village lads in stand-up collars and high crowned bowlers, small children of both sexes shrieking round the enclosures in skirts. The military band played stirring marches and Mr Alfred's private orchestra played Gilbert and Sullivan. There was bonhomie in the beer tent, banter and rivalry around the exhibits and finally everyone repaired to the main marquee for a luncheon.

Again the familiar sequence; Alfred's meat and wines, Alfred's cigars, Alfred's health repeatedly toasted, and an elegant little *ex cathedra* message penned from New Court and read out to resounding cheers.

In the afternoon the show judges deliberated on shire horses and hunters, pigs, Aylesbury ducklings and giant marrows . . . the list of prizes went on for columns. There were a military tournament, sideshows, trade exhibits and later a treat for those fortunate to have obtained tickets. They were admitted to the inner parklands around the mansion, where they wandered round the lake, the shrubberies, the Italian gardens and the fountains and water grottoes. They even stole glimpses of Alfred's treasures through the windows of the chateau.

On that last golden day of August 1913 the sun never shone brighter, the band of the Royal Horse Guards (swinging with selections from *Hello Ragtime*) never played merrier and the public luncheon never tasted better.

Agreed, there were undertones of anxiety among some of the servants and the tenants. What was going to happen at Halton when Mr Alfred finally passed to that last great heavenly playground in the sky? He was now in his 72nd year and known to be not too strong.

But when Lionel Rothschild, Alfred's nephew and MP for Aylesbury, read out his uncle's customary little message: 'Welcome you have always been, welcome you are and welcome you always will be!' they almost split the canvas roof off the marquee.

What after all was there to worry about? There was a new generation of nice young Rothschild nephews like Mr Lionel coming along, and an even younger generation behind them. The family had never failed to look after its people. Halton's future was secure.

That was 31 August 1913. Before the next show the following year, Britain was at war.

LEFT: Alfred's Rolls Royce, in the stable area at Halton; (BC) RIGHT: the pride of Alfred's car collection, a 1 ton Renault, on the terrace of Halton House; (HP) CENTRE: the fleet of an early motor car enthusiast: left to right — a 12 HP Wolseley, 18 HP Renault, 4 cylinder Zedel, another Renault and a 24 HP Elswick. The BH prefix indicates early Bucks registration; (HP) and BELOW: the five chauffeurs employed by Alfred Rothschild.
(BC)

OPPOSITE ABOVE: The private fire brigade at Halton, photographed in 1907 against the Chilterns; happily it never performed in earnest at Halton House; (HP) CENTRE: fire-fighting practice drill at Halton House before the 1914-18 war; (BC) BELOW: Frederick Hubbard, Alfred's agent at Halton, on a tour of inspection. (Note the AR monogram on the livery); (HP) ABOVE: the gentlefolk of Bucks relax around the ornamental lake, to the strains of a military band, at one of the annual agricultural shows, (BCRL) and BELOW: judging the livestock at one of the annual shows of the Chiltern Hills Agricultural Association, about 1900. (RG)

ABOVE: Harvesting scene at Halton before the Great War, (RG) and BELOW: the scale of Rothschild hospitality. In 1902, when this photo is believed to have been taken, Alfred invited the whole of Halton, Aston Clinton and Weston Turville to Coronation celebrations. (Women and children had a second sitting!) (RG)

68

ABOVE: Friendly cricket match between Halton and Wendover to celebrate Mr Alfred's 67th birthday in 1909. Frederick Hubbard, the agent, is rear centre, and Bob Sanders, head gardener, on his right. Alfred's pavilion and cricket ground are now a well known lawn tennis club; (RAFH) BELOW: Edwardian garden party in the Halton grounds; Alfred can be seen leaning forward to catch the camera. (HP)

LEFT: 'The best and kindest host in the world' (Disraeli) — Alfred Rothschild, caught in an informal mood; (BG) RIGHT: Lodge gates off Chestnut Drive, (HP) and BELOW: canal boating trip on the Wendover spur of the Grand Junction Canal; the bridge was the dividing line between the Halton and Aston Clinton estates. (RG)

70

ABOVE: The head gardener's house, with Mr Robert Sanders and his family, (ES) and BELOW: the Halton post-office, one of many older village buildings that were radically rebuilt in the Rothschild style. (MK)

ABOVE: Modern view of the Wendover spur, disused since the beginning of the century, as it passes Canal Cottage in Halton Village; (AA) BELOW: the village lane and canal bridge; (the Church lies to the right). The horse moved! (HP)

Golden days in Wendover, before its invasion by tens of thousands of Halton troops — ABOVE: The old village pump; (AK) CENTRE: The post office (right now the chemist's), (AK) and BELOW: Pound Street. (AK)

OPPOSITE ABOVE: High Street, Wendover; (AK) CENTRE: Coldharbour Cottages, (JM) and BELOW: the Rising Sun public house, on Upper Icknield Way; (RG) ABOVE: The end of an epoch, 1914: the unspoilt beauty of Halton Woods and Boddington Hill caught in this distant view from Bacombe Hill across Wendover. (JM)

WENDOVER AFTER THE WAR.

"The war has been a Godsend to Wendover."
Most of us have heard that remark made. We
question whether it is an altogether admirable comment. It sounds rather as if one were to say: "The
murder of my mother put a good two thousand pounds
into my pocket."

Still, one man's poison is another man's meat, and
Wendover as a community has done so well in sending
her sons to fight the country's battles, that her prosperity, even though it is only of a temporary nature,
may be looked upon as her deserved reward.

At the present moment many people who were only
earning fifteen shillings a week before the war are now
earning three times that amount. The presence of the

HERE, THERE, AND EVERYWHERE.

Walter Ratcliffe has been invalided home from the
Mediterranean.

* * * * * *

At the meeting in the School Yard at the beginning
of the war—a very memorable meeting in its way—
Walter Ratcliffe was the first Wendover man to come
forward to offer his services to his country. He was
closely followed by "Jimmy" Dorrell, if we remember
rightly.

* * * * * *

Wendover is not likely to forget the blizzard of the
28th—especially the special constables who were on
duty that night. We congratulate these men on the
prompt and uncomplaining way in which they turned
out. It was very far from being a joke.

* * * * * *

The road was blocked between World's End and
Stoke Turn by two fallen trees, and the drifts across
the roads were in several places two or three feet
deep. A large tree was blown down at the Vicarage.

* * * * * *

The "biscuit" goes this month to the lady who,
when it was pointed out to her that a blaze of light
came from the back premises of her house, contrary
to the lighting regulations, replied: "But I thought
it was only the front of the house that mattered!"

* * * * * *

The people of Wendover should note that the lighting restrictions are going to be enforced very strictly.

* * * * * *

Some arrangements might be made for the wives
and mothers who visit soldiers at the Camp. It was
pitiable on the night of the blizzard to see some of
these poor women, many of them with babies in their
arms, trying to find shelter. This seems a job for the
Recruiting and General Purposes Sub-Committee.

* * * * * *

Second-Lieut. Woollerton has been home from the
Front on leave, looking very fit and cheerful.

* * * * * *

As we go to press we learn with the deepest regret
that Second-Lieut. Edgar Smith, of the West Yorks,
has been dangerously wounded. We hope that the
report may turn out to be exaggerated.

* * * * * *

Before our next number the P.O. will be removed
to No. 1, London Road.

* * * * * *

The Wendover hay-tiers in khaki are: Sergt. W.
Edmonds, Pte. J. Atkins, Sergt. A. Edmonds, Pte.
W. Bishop, Sergt. F. Moore, Pte. E. Moore, Sergt.
B. Moore, Pte. W. Pedel, and Pte. W. Gorley. Quite
a family party!

LEFT: How it all began: Alfred making a personal visit in September 1913 to
the Brigade of Guards, who were his honoured (and pampered) guests at
Halton; (HP) RIGHT: Wendover goes to war, and BELOW: sadly recognises
the benefits — in the *Wendover Magazine* of April 1916.

Halton at War

'Of all the acres Rothschild owns
And there's many neat and smart
The one that is distinguished most
Is christened Halton Park.
There's five and twenty thousand
Bold recruits have made a start
To train to fight the Germans
In this glorious Halton Park'.

(Postcard verses by an anonymous Royal Northumberland Fusilier)

Halton's first encounter with khaki occurred in 1913 and, compared with the grim events of 1914 onwards, it was pure *opera bouffe.*

In September of that year Buckinghamshire and surrounding counties resounded to more martial activity than at any time since the Civil War. Besides the usual seasonal territorial training, 22,000 regulars poured into Buckinghamshire as part of the Army's summer manoeuvres. They all had to be quartered somewhere by the landowners of the shire.

Alfred unhesitatingly offered a portion of the Halton parklands to the military authorities and was given a tall order — the 1st Brigade of Guards under the command of Brigadier General Maxse. With their supply units and a few artillery they totalled 2,500 men. At this point anyone but a Rothschild would have locked up the house and maidservants and gone away for a week, having taken good note of the small print concerning compensation.

Not so Alfred. He determined that everything should be done to make the sojourn of both officers and men as commodious as possible.

His solution was hilariously unmilitary. Not only did the camp go up on the site of the Chiltern Hills Agricultural Show, (which had only just been dismantled) but he got back all the trappings of the show for the Guards. Back came James Putnam from Aylesbury with his enormous marquees and striped awnings and 60 workmen to erect them. Up rose a huge yellow and green mess tent for the 150 officers, leading off into a canvas anteroom dotted with settees, comfortable chairs and palm trees. Back came the civilian caterers with all their china and silver and 70 waiters and chefs for the officers alone.

And back trotted the three score Halton gardeners, who carefully arranged displays of flowers and shrubs around the marquees to beautify the scene. A local firm erected a battery of lamps to illuminate the camp lines at night.

The Brigade of Guards must have wondered what kind of clover they had stumbled into. When Alfred came down to see how they were getting on, the troops rose from their Rothschild rations of chicken, ham, hot pies, bread and butter, beer, tea, mineral waters and free tobacco as one man, and 'cheered as only Englishmen can'. (One soldier remarked 'You will readily understand that if we stayed here a solid month we should be too fat to march, let alone to walk'.)

77

Up the hill Alfred had yet more guests: No 3 Squadron of the newly formed Royal Flying Corps. During the manoeuvres, they were camped around the natural amphitheatre which one day would become the Maitland parade square; once cleared of sheep it made a passable aerodrome.

No 3 Squadron totalled 25 officers and 150 airmen under the command of Major Henry Brooke-Popham (later Air Chief Marshal). Among them was a young air mechanic, James McCudden, destined to become the greatest British air ace of the Great War, with 57 enemy aircraft kills. Brooke-Popham had less than a dozen unwieldy aircraft — Bleriot monoplanes, Renault BE biplanes and Henri Farman biplanes, with less than three hours' fuel and an average speed of 60 mph. Disaster was never very far away. One machine piloted by Lieutenant Wadham of the Hampshire Regiment was nearly written off in an overshoot.

The people of Buckinghamshire flocked to see the aviators at work. A contemporary photograph shows one of the Henri Farman machines in the 'aeroplane tents' being admiringly examined by a concourse of ladies and gentlemen in their Sunday best. One wonders if their enthusiasm would have been so great if they could see where it would all lead.

In the summer of 1914 the war clouds darkened and broke. Alfred, as we have seen, had played a small part behind the scenes in trying to avert the catastrophe.

Now, on the outbreak of hostilities, he lost no time in throwing open far wider portions of his parklands to the Army, on the sole condition that they were returned to him within six months of the end of war in *the same condition in which they were lent.*

This sole condition, which was an entirely reasonable protection for the owner, was destined to defeat his purpose and cause the destruction of the whole estate.

At the same time, Alfred's brother Nathaniel offered a training site on the adjoining estate and the Aston Clinton mansion was volunteered as a headquarters.

The Army accepted Halton with alacrity. The excellent rail and road links and the proximity of London made it an ideal place for concentrating or dispersing large bodies of men. Within a few weeks the South Staffordshire Territorials were billeted in Wendover for tent-pitching duties at Halton.

The initial occupants were the 21st Yorkshire Division, the senior formation of Kitchener's Third New Army. The division was raised in September 1914 and its various elements were at first billeted in the neighbourhood of Tring.

When the camp was prepared, the entire division marched into Halton Park, something like 12,000 men in a day. Seventy years later villagers recall their astonishment at the endless columns of tired, dusty men begging for cups of water.

Many of the fixed lines were on the present airfield. An enterprising photographer captured the scene from the roof of Halton Mansion for a picture postcard.

Spirits among the men in those early days of the war were high and, according to the poetical Northumbrian, the lads from Halton Park were going to show the Boche a thing or two:

> 'Then when Berlin is taken
> The Kaiser will remark,
> Where did those devils come from?
> The answer: Halton Park'.

Meanwhile the soldiers lived roughly in bell tents, slogging through musketry drill, bayonet drill, entrenching practice and route marches. The relics of these days — vast earthworks and rusting coils of barbed wire — still lie deep in the woods surrounding Halton.

The soldiers were not oblivious to the splendour of their surroundings:

> 'Then the sight at night is splendid,
> Especially after dark,
> When the tents are lit with candles,
> In this spacious Halton Park'.

However, the splendour evaporated in the foul weather of November as the camp became waterlogged. The infantry learned, like the airmen after them, that Halton in the wet abounded in 'mud of the chalky variety'.

The only people who came out of it reasonably comfortably were the divisional command, who had set up headquarters at the Aston Clinton mansion. The rest of the division was forced to return to billets scattered throughout Buckinghamshire and Hertfordshire.

During the winter, a large number of semi-permanent hutments were erected on three different sites. North Camp, accommodating 5,000 men, sprang up on part of Nathaniel's property, to the east of the Mansion. Alongside Upper Icknield Way and closer to Wendover was East Camp. It sprawled over the foot of the Chilterns above Main Point and held a further 5,000 men. On the other side of the Way, laid out on Clayfield, was West Camp, which held 2,000 men.

In February the Secretary of State for War, Lord Kitchener, whose famous pledge of 70 divisions had created all this endeavour, came down to inspect progress. In fact, Lord Kitchener's own hand may be discerned in the militarisation of Halton. Alfred had long been a close friend of the Field Marshal. Roth recounts that in the early part of the war he would call daily at the War Office and take him home for lunch at Seamore Place.

A few weeks later the 21st moved back into the new quarters.

Thus Halton Mansion and the inner parklands became an island ringed in a sea of khaki and canvas. Even then Alfred's legendary hospitality did not desert him, and there are members of those Yorkshire regiments who still recall the old-world dignity with which the household staff would bring an elegant tea and refreshments down to the officers.

The 21st division was composed entirely of Yorkshire and other northern battalions. Unfortunately none of these battalions published histories of their own, and the few references to Halton in regimental histories speak mainly of the rain and mud. After completing battalion training, the infantry moved, commencing on 9 August 1915, to Witley Camp and a month later the 'Kitcheners' were in France.

The impact of the first incursion upon the local communities had been nothing short of volcanic. Wendover took the brunt and after four months of war a resident wrote: 'Save for one or two events that tend to show that beneath the mud and broken roads our normal parish life continues somewhere, the war seems to have engulfed Wendover'.

Engulfed was the word. Robert Louis Stevenson's 'straggling, purposeless sort of place' had been jolted from its centuries-old charm and peace. It woke to the sound of bugles and shook to marching feet and rumbling lorries. Its hillsides were scarred with white gaping wounds. 'A new population fills our streets, young men, strong and sturdy and of strange tongue. We are proud of them and just a little afraid of them'.

TABLE

Battalions of the 21st Division which trained at Halton Park Camp, September '14-August '15:

62nd Brigade: 12th and 13th Northumberland Fusiliers
        8th East Yorks
        10th Green Howards
63rd Brigade: 14th Northumberland Fusiliers
        8th Lincolns
        12th West Yorks
        10th York and Lancs
64th Brigade: 9th and 10th King's Own Yorkshire Light Infantry
        14th and 15th Durham Light Infantry.

Afraid or not, Wendover was also discovering the compensations of a military town. The pages of the wartime *Wendover Magazine* were filled with advertisements for things for Tommy Atkins —

pipes, cigarettes, tobacco, Thorn's tonsorial parlour ('hair cuts and shaves'), the Corner House dining and tea rooms ('the soldiers' home from home'), khaki wool and clothes, black-out material, bootmakers, tailoring and so on. The presence of the camp produced new industries, the most profitable being laundering. The brewers worked all hours, the hotels were full, and rented houses were snapped up by wives and camp followers. By 1916 people who only earned 15 shillings a week before the war were getting three times that amount and, like it or not, the *Wendover Magazine* admitted that 'The war has been a godsend to Wendover'.

A mile away at Halton Camp the picture was different. Inexorably the Army began to spread out over the estate, eating up the Rothschild acres with the services necessary to keep thousands of men housed, fed and occupied in training. Roadways, paths, pipelines, parade grounds, sports grounds, rifle ranges, trenches, incinerators, rubbish tips, latrines and barbed wire transformed the face of Halton. Soon 700 acres were under direct military occupation.

(The systematic destruction of the estate was colourfully described by AVM Sir Philip Game after the war. 'When I first saw it [Halton] closely in 1914 there was nothing here except a house and 7,000 pheasants which no doubt the New Army ate . . . I did not see it again until 1919. There was nothing here then except workshops and a sea of wooden huts.')

Noone has calculated precisely the number of soldiers who trained at the Halton camps during the recruiting bulge of 1914-1916. One or two unofficial sources suggest as many as 25,000, but that may have been partly a propaganda figure. Divisional strength was around 12,000 men and, in addition, there were other support services and lodger units. There was also a satellite camp at Hale Field camp two miles away. Probably a figure of between 15,000 and 20,000 men would be more accurate.

Thus for a time Halton was one of the major military camps in the country. The pinnacles of Halton Mansion, and the parklands churned to white mud, were among the last memories of England that those battalions carried away, as they marched off to be slaughtered like cattle in the trenches. We cannot follow all their fortunes here, but the sacrifice of the Yorkshire lads at the Battle of the Somme, among the useless carnage of the whole war, should be remembered.

The 21st was one of 14 divisions which went over the top near Fricourt on 1 July 1916. The attack followed a continuous artillery barrage lasting six days and nights, which was supposed to have knocked out the German resistance but failed utterly. The German machine gunners emerged from their deep shelters and mowed down the British and French troops like wheat. 19,000 British soldiers died on the first day alone, most of them between 0730 and 0800. Of those, no less than 4,265 were men of the 21st Division.

After the Yorkshiremen had left Halton, the East Anglian regiments arrived, and the process of converting raw recruits into trained but untried soldiers for the drafts to France, Gallipoli and Mesopotamia started all over again. A bundle of faded letters written in pencil from Hut 37 in C Lines of West Camp by young Private Arthur Patrick of the Northamptonshire Regiment has been preserved by his family. The letters convey vividly the fears, the frustration and the tedium of the East Anglian lads as they trained for their turn in 'the big show'.

Throughout the spring and summer of 1916 they alternately shivered and sweated as they learned the grim new science of trench warfare. On the Chiltern slopes they added to the trench systems left by the 21st Division, practising saps and mines and live bomb throwing. They strung miles of barbed wire, laid dummy minefields and learned the savage skills of bayonetry. They fired countless rounds into the rifle ranges against the foot of the Chilterns and carried out mass company attacks. Their feet and their shoulders grew calluses from route marches and parade ground drill.

At night, they suffered the boredom of sentry and fire picquet duties and standing guard. Reveille woke them to the tyranny of the daily hut inspection, when the orderly officer expected the hut to look 'like a house after spring cleaning'; for those on standby for the draft there was a full daily kit inspection.

Morale was good, sustained by letters, parcels and newspapers sent from home and by the natural camaraderie of the county regiments. Until later in the year there was a relative ignorance of the hell ahead of them. In the evenings and at weekends they relaxed, with inter-company cricket, singsongs and beer at the YMCA and walking out into Wendover. There were occasional leave passes too, for those whose movements were not interrupted by epidemics of measles, impetigo and other infectious diseases, for Halton was an unhealthy camp.

Yet over it all lay the dread of what lay ahead, which increased as the magnitude of the death toll on the Somme became obvious from the newspapers. In young Arthur Patrick, as in so many of his fellows, bravery was mixed with resignation. 'Tell Mother not to start worrying about it', he wrote to his sister about being drafted overseas; 'for she must have realized by now, as I have done, that it must be the ultimate end of our training. I hope we shall do our duty as so many have already done. As the poet says "What is to be done will be and there's an end on't".'

In August came the finale. They were put on draft and underwent two big inspections by visiting Generals in quick succession. On 9 August in sweltering heat they mounted a mock attack on Coombe Hill. There was free beer one evening and the next day they marched out of their lines for the last time. Arthur Patrick went to France in September and was dead by Christmas. He died, not of wounds but, like so many others, from pneumonia caught in the appalling conditions of winter in the trenches.

That winter Halton suffered another savage piece of destruction and ironically it was of Alfred Rothschild's own making. While giving unstintingly of his time to advise the Treasury on financing the war, Alfred felt he ought to do more to help the country. In the winter of 1916-17 the Government faced a critical shortage of timber, and on 28 February 1917 Alfred wrote to Lloyd George, the Prime Minister:

'I am, I must confess, not an expert as regards what sort of timber would be suitable for "pit props", but I cannot help thinking that, as there are so many fine trees in my woods at Halton, some of them at least would be suitable . . . May I ask you very kindly to send down your expert who would very easily be able to report fully on the subject, and I should be indeed very proud if my offer should lead to any practical result.'

There is pathos about the patriotism of the old man as he volunteered his magnificent beechwoods to the voracious war machine. The Government lacked good hardwood for everything from building to aeroplane spares and duckboard for the trenches. In no time at all Canadian lumberjacks were sought out from the Expeditionary Force in France and drafted to Halton.

There they fell on the woods above Icknield Way with the joyous enthusiasm of men newly released from the trenches. The hillside rang with the sound of axes and crashing trees. The lumberjacks' techniques were un-English, and the locals were horrified to see trees felled at shoulder height, leaving great stumps like rows of bared teeth. A narrow gauge railway was built to extract the timber to Wendover station.

By this time the military importance of Halton was declining. In December 1916 it lost divisional status and became merely brigade strength. From October it was also the Eastern Command Reserve Centre, commanded by Brigadier General J. E. Bush. According to the *Official Short History of the RAF* (1929) one of the units under his command was a Royal Flying Corps recruit training centre.

This is the first mention of the wartime khaki and putteed airmen at Halton, with their funny 'maternity jacket' tunics, which led local villagers to confuse them with German prisoners-of-war. Like a small cloud on the horizon, their arrival at the end of 1916 presaged great changes to come.

ABOVE: View from the roof of Halton House, August 1914. The first units of the 21st Division of Kitchener's Third New Army are encamped on what later became the airfield, (HP) and CENTRE: the same view today. Parked aircraft and hangars can be seen above the trees; (AA) BELOW: The tented camps grow. (This was East Camp, near the present Maitland Square area). (HA)

ABOVE: 'A pretty woodland scene at Wendover', 1914 — This picture postcard tranquility was soon to be shattered; CENTRE: between East Camp and the Weston Turville reservoir semi-permanent huts sprang up; (RG) BELOW: these ugly wooden huts, housing 24 men each, soon covered the Halton pastures. Ablutions and cookhouses are in the foreground. (RE)

THE LADS FROM HALTON PARK.

Of all the acres Rothschild owns,
  And there's many neat and smart,
The one that is distinguished most
  Is christened Halton Park.

There five and twenty thousand,
  Bold recruits have made a start,
To train to fight the Germans,
  In this glorious Halton Park.

Up early in the morning,
  They go, singing like the lark,
To fetch their steaming cocoa,
  From the cookhouses, Halton Park.

Then the sight at night is splendid,
  Especially after dark,
When the tents are lit with candles,
  In this spacious Halton Park.

And when they're trained and ready,
  For the Front they will embark ;
You will hear the people shouting,
  There's the lads from Halton Park

Then when Berlin is taken,
  The Kaiser will remark,
Where did those demons come from ?
  The answer : Halton Park.

When our arms have been victorious,
  And each man has made his mark,
Where will the highest honours go ?
  To the lads from Halton Park.

G.P.

(A Northumberland Fusilier).

October 19th, 1914.

OPPOSITE ABOVE: East camp in summer 1915, transformed by wooden and tin huts; the building on the right is officers' accommodation; (SP) BELOW and ABOVE: The spirit of Tommy Atkins ran high at Halton in the early days of the war. These jingoistic post cards were designed to cheer up the folks at home. (AK)

MORGAN'S,

AT THE

Clock Tower

THE BEST PLACE FOR

TOBACCO

AND

CIGARETTES,

AND ALL THE

BEST MAKES OF

CHOCOLATES.

BAKER OF MORGAN'S

Pure Home-made Bread.

STATIONERY

—AND—

FANCY GOODS.

THORN'S
Tonsorial Parlour.

HAIR CUTTING and SHAVING

AT MODERATE PRICES.

— ALL THE BEST BRANDS OF —

Tobacco, Cigarettes and Cigars.

The Most Convenient Place
for Soldiers.

Mr. F. J. Thorn's premises are close to the Clock
Tower in
AYLESBURY STREET.

—THE—

Temperance Hotel,

AYLESBURY STREET.

The best place for Soldiers
For TEAS and DINNERS.

Comfortable Rooms.
Excellent Cooking.
Admirable Service.

Very Comfortable Bedrooms and Excellent Hotel
Arrangements.
MODERATE CHARGES.

TOBACCO, CIGARETTES, CIGARS.

The Best Milk in Wendover Supplied Daily.

Mrs. NORTH, Proprietress.

Local advertisers tempt the troops in the November 1916 *Wendover Magazine.*

3 and 5, High Street, WENDOVER.

Protect yourself from the Zeppelins

by coming to

NICHOLAS LEE'S

for your dark

Blinds and Casement Curtains,

which are procurable in any shade, cheap and thoroughly reliable.

We have already executed large orders for the Camps at Halton Park, so take our advice and ensure your safety by using our Curtains.

We must not forget during the present crisis that Tommy still welcomes presents of

Tobacco & Cigarettes,

and all kinds of comforts which he is unable to obtain for himself, but which we are selling at the

MOST POPULAR PRICES.

JUST RECEIVED !

100 Yards Green Lightproof Window Holland, 36 inches wide, to be cleared at **6d. per yard.** *Very Special.*

LEFT: Bomb scare and business — *Wendover Magazine,* April 1916; ABOVE: infantry officers relaxing outside a fairly capacious mess; (SP) CENTRE: interior of an officer's hut at Halton with cot bed and small writing desk, (SP) and BELOW: wartime YMCA notice in Wendover. (The club was not in the old school house seen on the left, but further down the lane). (AK)

ABOVE: 'We had some jolly good times in Hut 37 I can assure you. I've always enjoyed myself'. Pte Arthur Patrick is third from right in the middle row; (AK) BELOW: D Company, 3/4 Battalion, Northamptonshire Regiment, on parade for the photographers. (AK)

ABOVE: Halton rifle ranges, 1915, at the foot of the Chiltern escarpment;
(SP) BELOW: the spoils of war: captured German guns at Halton Camp.
(RAFH)

For God, For King & For Country.

Y·M·C·A
H.M. FORCES ON ACTIVE SERVICE

Y.M.C.A.

Y.M.C.A.

PATRON
Y.M.C.A. NATIONAL COUNCIL.
H.M. THE KING.

PATRON
MILITARY CAMP DEPT.
H.R.H. DUKE OF CONNAUGHT.

Reply to .... Company .... Bat ...... Regt. ......   June 18th   1915

Stationed at   Halton Park
                Bucks

Dear Mother,

Just a line hoping you are quite well. Thank
Maggie for her letter I see Ed has got off a bit longer then Jo he still at
Geddington? if he is he'll have a middling time I'll bet.

I was on Guard Barrack Store Guard last night – Its only from 5.30
to 6.30 this morning we only have this Guard when we are doing brigade
duties. What do you think of the enclosed photo it comprises the biggest part
of D. Co. We had took one day on the parade ground the officers quarters are in
the background. We had four new chaps come on our hut on Friday –
they are all home service men – one of them used to be foreman gardener
at Rockingham Castle, they were in the last few groups I think.

Thanks for butter which I have just received I see Aunt Lizzie
escaped the arm of the law, the dog has caused a lot of trouble.

Well I don't think I've got much more to say
so I will close
– with love to all
from your loving
Arthur

Letters home: there were YMCA huts at each camp and in Wendover and
Aston Clinton, where the men could relax, play billiards and hear concerts.
(AK)

90

Enter the Airmen!

'The Adjutant General is at his wits' end to find *men*, let alone skilled mechanics . . . neither the Master General for Ordnance nor the Quartermaster General know where to look for the necessary skilled artificers.'
Director of Air Organization to General Trenchard in France, August 1917.

The value of air power was finally brought home to the General Staff by the undisputed air mastery which Trenchard won over the trenches during the first part of the Somme offensive. At the start of 1917, the Army Council approved on paper the expansion of the RFC to the staggering size of 106 battle and 97 reserve squadrons. This was an increase of 57 squadrons altogether; where on earth were they to come from?

The limiting factor was neither fresh pilots nor fresh aircraft, though there was severe concern about their quality. (In April 1917 pilots were being posted to the front with as little as 17.5 hours' instruction and their life expectancy had shortened proportionately: 92 flying hours on average before death or injury compared with 295 hours in August 1916.) The problem lay with the ground support, for it took 17 men (or women) to keep one training aircraft in the air, and no less than 47 for a fighting machine. The most pressing shortage was of air mechanics, whom Trenchard keenly appreciated were 'the backbone of all our efforts'.

It was unfortunate that the Army, ever suspicious of the demands of its youngest progeny, faced identical problems at this juncture. For did not the engineers, the service corps, and above all the artillery need skilled mechanics just as urgently to win the war on the ground?

As the Adjutant-General himself wrote witheringly: 'If the RFC are to be given precedence we shall probably collapse in some other direction'. More planes unavoidably meant less artillery firepower.

But that was only part of the Corps' dilemma. The 'skilled artificers' so essential to the squadrons were a new breed of which the Army knew little: aeroengine fitters on whom the efficiency of the temperamental aircraft depended, general fitters, erectors, coppersmiths to repair pipe lines, tinsmiths and sheet metal workers for the engine cowlings, blacksmiths for tool making, vulcanisers, riggers, who were variously carpenters, sailmakers and wire stringers who repaired the battle-torn fuselages and wings, and magneto repairers. (The fact that the British aircraft industry in 1914 was almost entirely dependent on Germany for its supply of magnetos proved a serious wartime embarassment.)

Early in the war the Flying Corps had reached an obvious conclusion. Once it had combed the other Services and Civvy Street for the small pool of skilled men available, it had to start training its own mechanics — and to do so in ever increasing numbers.

According to the official war history, recruiting was adequate until the vast expansion of the Corps in 1916, but mechanic training was scattered in an uncoordinated fashion over the country. It ranged from Netheravon (200 men) and Reading (1,000) to a jam factory at nearby Coley

(2,000), commercial premises in Edinburgh (300) and barracks at Curragh.

Moreover the Corps had no basic engineering course for semi-skilled recruits. In spring 1916 emergency arrangements were made (without Treasury permission) for 400 airmen to attend various polytechnics for eight weeks at 10s 6d per week. The headquarters of the scheme was the Regent Street Polytechnic, which also operated a recruiting service (at a shilling per man) through its industrial contacts.

Jam factories! Other ranks at polytechnics! Recruiting by civilians! Even the War Office agreed that improvisation had gone far enough. In June 1917 Sefton Branker, Deputy Director General of Military Aeronautics, submitted proposals to coordinate the technical training of men, women and boys in a new school which would also absorb the polytechnic scheme.

Halton was suggested because of its closeness to London and excellent transport links. The hutted accommodation and camp services, which by the end of 1917 had cost the Army £400,000, would with certain additions solve the Corps' needs at a stroke.

The Army was not overjoyed at losing its facilities but the entry of the United States into the war had removed the pressure from infantry training. In any event the RFC's needs could not be denied and in July 1917, they were again staggeringly increased; the War Cabinet authorised *doubling* the operational squadrons to 200, with comparable expansion of the reserve squadrons. This gigantic order (accompanied by a similar one for the Royal Naval Air Service) was unrealistic and never came near fulfilment. But it indicates the degree of urgency surrounding the change in Halton's role. The 1917 aviation budget voted £100,000 for permanent workshops at Halton to accommodate the Corps' multifarious mechanical trades.

In the summer of 1917 the infantry marched out of their lines at Halton to make room for the air mechanics. The East Anglian Territorial Brigade was one of the last to go, moving to Crowborough towards the end of the year. The fitters arrived in August and most of the riggers, together with the headquarters staff from the Reading school, in September.

The new school, named the School of Technical Training (Men) was under the direct control of the War Office, an indication of the importance of the new venture. Its first commanding officer was 34-year-old Lt Col Ian Bonham-Carter, who drove himself and everyone around him with relentless energy.

Bonham-Carter's background is of interest, since he was to return to command Halton between 1928 and 1931. As a Royal Northumberland Fusilier he had seen action in South Africa and North West India and, when serving with the first battalion, had acquired a reputation as the smartest adjutant in the British army.

His perseverance was legendary. After being seconded to the RFC in early 1914, Lieutenant Bonham-Carter gained his wings and flew with No 5 Squadron to France in August. The Fusiliers' regimental history mentions that he was forced down by bad weather on an early mission near Rozoy. By luck his old battalion was moving up to the line and a cheerful reunion took place. Soon afterwards, finding that the shortage of aircraft made life intolerably dull, he obtained permission to rejoin his old battalion temporarily. It was a bad exchange, for he was seriously wounded and had a leg amputated.

Undaunted, he returned to the Flying Corps and modified an aircraft so he could operate the rudder with a wheel and pulley mounted on top of the joystick! However the Corps had other ideas and, as commanding officer first at Reading then Halton, he made a reputation as a firm but fair disciplinarian with a gift for improvisation. He had need of such qualities. Halton was a mixed command of 6,000 airmen mechanics, 2,000 boys at the Boys Training Depot at West Camp, 1,700 instructors and administrators and — creating a dynamite situation — 2,000 women under training. These girls were trained in a variety of trades including riggers, electricians and painters. Though no airwomen served overseas during the war, over 300 served with the Air Force of Occupation at Cologne afterwards.

Living conditions for the RFC boy mechanics, the forerunners of Trenchard's RAF 'brats', were as spartan and unhealthy as for the infantry before them. Sixty years later S.E. Townson (retired Wing Commander) remembered the bucket sanitation, the open air ablutions which froze solid in the winter, the straw palliases on trestle beds, the prison-type hair cuts and the discipline 'more in keeping with a military detention barracks than preparation for a technical career'. The boys were permanently hungry, and the cookhouses each served upwards of 1,000 on a take-it-or-leave-it basis.

The winter of 1917-18 was exceptionally severe, and the crowded living conditions caused huge epidemics of infectious diseases. First individial boys, then entire huts, and then finally the different camps were isolated from the outside world. Community life ceased and coloured tabs were sewn onto the backs of the boys' tunics to identify the disease from which they were suffering (red for scarlet fever, blue for measles, white for mumps etc). Boys with similar colours were allowed to visit the canteens together for brief periods in the evening.

Bonham-Carter also had a small but energetic lodger unit of the Australian Flying Corps, which set up a training and supply depot at East Camp in September 1917. As well as spanking drill and discipline taught by Chelsea-trained NCOs, Australian mechanics received instruction at the new school. By the end of 1918, over 1,200 trained mechanics had been posted out to Australian squadrons, mostly in the Middle East. The supply depot had also received, equipped and reposted some 9,500 airmen newly arrived off the troopships.

It is pleasant to record that not everything at Halton was grim preparation for war. Bonham-Carter encouraged inter-unit sports and there was a busy calendar. The tough colonial unit, which was only 400 strong, had a remarkable record. In the winter of 1917-18 it carried off the inter-unit rugby, the soccer and the boxing trophies against huge numerical odds and posting notices. Next September it demolished the first RAF sports meeting at Halton, winning seven of the nine events. 'We regret to say that the RAF were rather hurt about this', recorded an Australian serviceman; 'and at a subsequent meeting . . . the Australians were not invited to enter'.

At first the training facilities for the RFC air mechanics were poor: a collection of small huts and assorted equipment. But by November 1917 the foundations of the huge workshop block were laid. Work proceeded rapidly as German prisoners-of-war laboured under the sharp-eyed direction of Colonel L. Sadler, the school's technical commandant.

The block, which has lasted 60 years surprisingly unchanged, covered 300,000 square feet and was built in twelve great bays, each 50 feet wide and 500 feet long. Each bay was designed to accommodate a different speciality: £250,000 worth of instructional machinery was ordered and, as each bay was completed, the men moved in.

Wartime training was by intensive 'crash courses'. Though programmes varied at different times, blacksmiths and electricians trained on average for 14 weeks, magneto repairers for 10 and aero fitters for eight. Some trades received only six weeks' specialised training. The demands of the squadrons were so acute that often it was impossible for a man to complete his training before his posting to France, Egypt or Mesopotamia.

Thus a year before the war ended Halton was pouring out mechanics in huge numbers: no less than 14,000 in 1917 alone. The deployment of the RFC mechanics to the operational squadrons overseas was greatly assisted by the loan of 15,000 American mechanics, who served with the RFC on home stations. This contribution to Britain's air power was of vital importance and helped directly towards ending the war, unlike the earlier slaughter of thousands of Halton-trained lads in the trenches.

The debt was clearly and repeatedly acknowledged by experts in military aviation during the negotiations which loomed over Halton's future after the war. It is to those negotiations that we now turn.

ABOVE: Airmen of the Royal Flying Corps in their 'maternity jackets'. From their cheerful expression they may well be marching to a Church parade; (MoD) BELOW: a rare photograph of the workshops in the No 1 School of Technical Training in the building. The labourers in the foreground are German prisoners of war. (RE)

ABOVE: The workshops completed. Note the descriptions on the first two bays, (shops for acetylene welders and coppersmiths); (EB) BELOW: interior of the workshops. A class of aircraft riggers undergo instruction at Halton in 1917. Note the overhead panels of enemy aircraft markings. (EB)

ABOVE: Australian aero engine fitters under instruction. At their peak, the workshops poured out 14,000 aircraft mechanics in 4 months of 1917; (EB)
BELOW: Aircraft on the Halton airfield, a wartime 'acceptance park'. Left to right: a BE 2c, a RE8 and a FE 28. The pilot of this FE 28 was later killed in a dog fight. The plane continued flying and the observer managed to kick down the partition and land by operating the controls while lying on the floor. (EB)

96

LEFT: Sergeant Street, and BELOW: 'My old Bus', his early Henri Farman
machine, flown at Halton, (AS) and RIGHT: Sports Day at Halton, summer
1917. The first commandant of the School of Technical Training, Lt Col Ian
Bonham-Carter, (right) prepares to give out the prizes. With him is one of
his staff officers, Major Nixon. (EB)

ABOVE: Some of the motor transport pool at Halton in 1917 (EB) and
BELOW: the Staff vehicles of the Australian Flying Corps unit, which
include a Minerva car and a Ford van. On the right is Lt Bowden. The lady
on the left (his driver) later became his wife. (EB)

Viewing the destruction of Halton's beechwoods. The group of workers and spectators includes several 'Land Girls', with Australian airmen in close attendance and German prisoners-of-war in working fatigues. (RE)

ABOVE: Airmen's cookhouse at Hale Field Camp, with cast iron range and water heaters; (EB) BELOW: summer 1917. Frederick Hubbard, Alfred's ageing agent, and other Rothschild retainers watch the station sports at Halton's ruined fields. There is sadness and regret on every face. (EB)

Exit the Rothschilds

'Where are the Greuzes, the Nattiers, the Watteaus, that smiled down from those exquisitely lit up walls? And where the years of the lavish taste and planning of this home of a childless man?' — *The Countess of Warwick (1931)*

The process whereby Halton Park passed from the Rothschilds into the less gentle hands of the War Office has been obscured by the passing years. One modern version is that Alfred chivalrously presented the entire estate to the hard-pressed Government as a gift. The other is that the War office, armed with emergency powers, imposed compulsory purchase and Alfred promptly died of a broken heart.

The truth, as so often happens, is not so romantic. While an undoubted patriot, Alfred Rothschild was not so self-sacrificing, nor was Whitehall so powerful. In fact, the War Office's haunting fear was that it had started to build the School of Technical Training on land specifically *exempted* from the Defence of the Realm (Land Acquisition) Regulations.

The facts of the affair lie in dusty Air Ministry files which were only opened to the public in the 1970s. They tell a sorry tale, in which the Rothschilds appear in a far better light than either the Government or the fledgling Royal Air Force.

The tale starts in Autumn 1917, when Lloyd George's war cabinet accepted the recommendations of the Smuts Committee on the future of Britain's air power. When Parliament convened in October — to the chastening sounds of Gotha bombers raiding London at night — it was to introduce an Air Force Bill at top speed. The controversial 'separate service' was on its way at last.

The winter of 1917-18 was a desperate time for a major re-organisation within the armed forces; Trenchard himself had the gravest doubts about it, fearing that the efficiency of the fighting squadrons might be crippled.

In the midst of all its other preoccupations the Air Board had to take stock of its present and future needs, its flying stations, repair shops, depots, 'acceptance parks' (stations equipped to receive and prove aircraft fresh from the factories) and above all its training facilities. It also had to consider all the support services previously provided by the Army, from transport to hygiene and from rations to padres.

In the midst of this ferment of planning it became clear to somebody at the Air Board that Halton was anything but a granite rock upon which to be building a vital technical training school. Held on a gentleman's agreement with a 76-year-old patriot millionaire — now failing in health — it could prove a fearful pitfall. According to the terms of Alfred's offer in 1914, the new Service might be out on its ear six months after peace was signed.

There was only one answer: to purchase the Halton estate. The Air Board, however, lacked the jurisdiction for major land purchases and the Army Council, about to wash its hands of aviation problems, was disinclined to get involved.

On 12 November 1917 a cogent case was put up by Sir Paul Harvey, Secretary of the Air Board, to the War Office, urging the purchase of the Halton estate (which was incorrectly estimated at about 4,000 acres). The reasons given seemed straightforward: the imperative need to secure the Army's investment in bricks and mortar; Halton's communication and transport facilities which were 'of the very best', and the possibility of Halton Mansion itself becoming the Cadet College of the Royal Air Force.

However, a hidden memorandum brought out less reputable arguments for purchase, including the advisability of negotiating with the present owner 'whose patriotism and interest in the Army Air Services is well known'. This was smarter than deferring the matter to his successors who might be less public spirited — and tougher negotiators.

The argument for purchasing the estate in its entirety was questionable, but the Air Board in 1918 appeared haunted by the improvidence of the Boards of Admiralty in the 18th century, who dallied over purchasing dockyards and ended up by buying land piecemeal and expensively. The Air Board's proposal was to buy widely at cheap wartime rates and to lease or sell what was not immediately required. With the technical school set for expansion and additional roles for Halton being discussed — as a Staff College, Air Cadet College or the RAF's permanent depot — the future of the station could be exciting. The Air Board wanted room to match its designs.

At the War Office however, more cautious views prevailed, and the original proposal was watered down. The proposal addressed to the Lords Commissioners of the Treasury on 31 December 1917 was to purchase only 1,340 acres at a maximum of £50,000.

Some days later, against expectation and to the consternation of the Air Board, the Treasury rejected the application as 'case unproven'. Then a far more serious setback occurred: Alfred Rothschild died. He had lived too long and seen too much. His cousin Constance Battersea was sure that the war itself had hastened his death. 'He seemed very hopeless and dejected from the start' she wrote; 'and the fact of the cleavage that it [the war] had necessarily caused our once so united family must have caused poignant grief to his affectionate heart.'

He died at Seamore Place on 31 January 1918, having been confined to his home for some weeks, and he was buried at the Willesden Jewish cemetery. The event coincided with 14 tons of German bombs being dropped on Paris and his obituary notices were (for a Rothschild) no more than cursory.

The fear of Alfred's death had dogged the supporters of the Halton purchase, particularly Sir Howard Frank, the head of the Lands Directorate of the War Office and Ministry of Munitions. He was convinced that the Government had no compulsory powers to buy the land on which they were erecting the School of Training.

Worse still, he foresaw a nightmarish situation arising over compensation and reparations. Writing to the Parliamentary Under-Secretary on the day of Alfred's death, Frank emphasised 'it must be recognised that by erecting these buildings [ie the workshops] in this position . . . you have seriously damaged the amenities of Halton as a residential and sporting estate and I am afraid that the owner would be able to substantiate a considerable claim on this account alone'.

That was precisely how the new owner, Major Lionel de Rothschild, the elder son of Alfred's brother Leopold, saw the matter. Why should he part with a slice of the cake when the Government had ruined the whole confection? For the Air Board the Halton purchase had to be all or nothing, and nothing would be a very costly retreat.

A round of hasty meetings between the Parliamentary Under-Secretary and interested parties followed. In the event it was financial considerations which clinched the matter. On the one hand Lionel de Rothschild's valuation on the whole property (3,014 acres) was £168,100 inclusive of standing timber. He was however prepared to offer it to HM Government at £150,000, reserving only the rights of the Rothschild tenants.

Against that, Frank estimated the maximum inclusive market value at £95,000 — a niggardly sum. If, however, the sale did not go through, the Government would lose the training school

(£125,000 to date) and roadways, services and other buildings which ran into hundreds of thousands. They would also have to pay £50,000 for reinstatement and depreciation. Nor did these figures include the cost of returning the site of the North camp to the plough.

Military needs might ebb and flow but these were facts which their Lordships at the Treasury could not ignore. In April the Director General of Lands was authorised to seek immediate purchase at £95,000 exclusive, or if he thought he could drive a better bargain at a maximum all-in figure of £125,000.

With this authority Frank went off to treat with the Rothschilds and he drove a thunderingly hard bargain. On 29 May 1918 he reported the terms of sale to the Air Council: £112,000 for the 3,014 acre estate, which included the mansion, Halton village, the lodges and farms, all the timber and fixed machinery. Lionel had nine months after completion to remove Alfred's treasures from the Mansion and whatever fixtures he wanted.

It was, in Howard Frank's smug words 'an uncommonly good investment' and as Trenchard agreed at a later date, 'we got the estate very cheap'. Before the ink was dry on the contract, Frank was arranging to cut and sell the timber and calculating how much unwanted land he could put up for sale.

Thus the rape of Alfred's pastoral paradise was completed. The gentlemen soldiers he had admitted to his beloved parks had turned into monsters of desecration, whose masters offered baubles in recompense.

On one point only did Frank appear generous. To speed matters up the Lands Directorate promised to pay £1,000 towards the cost of removal from Halton Mansion, to classify the operation as an official priority and to provide lorries. It looked a fairly handsome disturbance allowance for 1918, but the DGL could afford it. The final stinginess was that he insisted that the Government be *paid* for the loan of the lorries.

Why, one may ask, was Lionel de Rothschild so compliant? Had the Rothschilds, who had driven razor-deals with every government in Europe, lost their touch? Indeed, why did the nephew sell at all, let alone in such haste? Alfred's will, dated as recently as 18 September 1917, clearly did not envisage the sale of Halton. The estate was entailed through some fifteen male heirs and brought with it all the precious contents and fittings (apart from the specific art bequests) and a £25,000 trust fund to be devoted to the maintenance and upkeep of the place.

One does not have to look far for answers. The Great War had done more than murder the flower of a generation: it had tilted the economic basis of British society. It had crippled private banking, the key to the Rothschild's fortunes. Furthermore, the death of three brothers within three years had robbed the family of leadership and left it reeling from death duties.

There was a new economic climate about. The old Edwardian pretensions had gone and with them would go many great London homes and country seats. Lionel had no interest in maintaining Halton as a gilded monument to his uncle's memory. His eyes were turning to a 2,600 acre estate at Exbury in the New Forest, which he bought the following year.

The other influencing factor, perhaps, was the revelation of what Alfred had done with the rest of his £2.5 million estate. Since Alfred had no wife nor little Rothschildren to provide for, family usage required a rigid transference of his wealth inside the family. Instead, after a generous list of bequests to friends, servants and relatives, he left Seamore Place with its fabulous paintings and furnishing and a large cash sum to Almina, Countess of Carnarvon.

This fortunate young woman was young enough to be Alfred's daughter, which is precisely what she proved to be. Further instructions in the will revealed that he had previously settled £500,000 on her wedding settlement; this sum was still being paid off at his death.*

So Alfred's little secret — or one of them — was out. Almina's mother was a Frenchwoman, Marie Felice Boyer. After their affair she was married to Captain Frederick Charles Wombwell, fourth son of a Yorkshire baronet.

Alfred's death had a further fascinating epilogue. Almina's inheritance financed Lord Carnarvon's last and most famous expedition, to the Valley of the Kings near ancient Thebes. There in November 1922 Rothschild money struck gold once more, the fabulous treasures of Tutankamun.

In February 1923 the great burial chamber was unsealed, but in the hour of his triumph Lord Carnarvon was struck down, dying mysteriously of a respiratory illness at Cairo in April. For years the Curse of the Pharaohs was seriously implied even by intelligent people. Had the ancient god-kings who enslaved the Hebrews in Egypt taken revenge on the noblemen who used Jewish wealth to disturb their peace? The ending, though grim, was nicely rounded.

Today some medical historians have a different theory. The Earl's symptoms are consistent with pulmonary histoplasmosis, an infection which he might have contracted by inhaling particles of bat faeces when he entered the underground passages leading to the tomb.

But this is to leap ahead. By late summer of 1918 Lionel Rothschild had completed his sacrificial negotiations with the War Office and the last Rothschild carriage rumbled away from Halton Park. A mammoth party marked the end of an era; legend has it that when the Air Ministry took over on 29 September 1918 they found empty champagne bottles in every room and the swimming pool in the basement swirling with flat champagne.

---

* Alfred's relations with the Carnarvons have the flavour of a French novel. He was in the congregation in June 1895 when Almina married George Herbert, the fifth Earl of Carnarvon at St Margaret's, Westminster. The bride was given away by an older Wombwell, while her mother's husband Captain Frederick Wombwell and her lover Alfred looked on. The young couple were fond and frequent visitors to Alfred's homes and the Earl, who was a celebrated Egyptologist, took Alfred wintering to Egypt to see his excavations. Marie, who died a rich woman in 1913, left *articles de vertu* to her old lover and to his brother Leopold.

The Rothschild home at Aston Clinton, once owned by Alfred's uncle Sir Anthony de Rothschild. After loaning it to the Army as a divisional HQ, the owners were cruelly repaid. The building was demolished in the 1960s.
(NMR)

'A pocket Venus who stood out from her contemporaries'. The lovely
Almina, Countess of Carnavon, as described by her son; sketch by P. Helleu.
(KD)

105

ABOVE: Post war building continues (1922). The remains of the wartime West Camp can just be seen in the distance; (RAFH) BELOW: saved from the axe. Halton House, now an RAF Officers' Mess, seen from the air in 1927. Beyond are some of the huts of the wartime North Camp. (RAFH)

The Troubled Succession

'Wonderful old place in its way', said the Quartering Commandant;
'pity to knock it about too much.' *Brideshead Revisited*.

Though the Halton estate had been ravaged almost beyond recognition by the military between 1914 and 1918, Halton Mansion was more fortunate. It came to the RAF like an aging virtuous bride, heavily gilded but still intact.

This was simply because the mansion and inner grounds had remained Alfred's sanctuary. Veterans of the RFC have recalled him being driven around the estate in an open carriage in the winter of 1917-18, a frail little figure clutching a stick and swathed in furs like a Russian count.

So it was that when the men from the Ministry arrived at the chateau with their clipboards and pencils to make inventories, they entered like Visigoths capturing the unsacked Eternal City and wandered round gaping at its treasures.

From their report it is clear that Lionel Rothschild had been exceedingly liberal in what he left behind. The chandeliers, the silk blinds, the massive gilt mirrors, the bookcases in the library, the mouldings remained. More remarkable were the silk tapestries which adorned the walls of no less than 24 rooms and were estimated to cover some 5,000 square yards. In 1918, brilliant and unmarked, they were worth 'several thousand pounds' and were only outshone by the gilt and oak panelling of the Billiards Room, on which the Ministry men could not even put a figure.

There was also the beautiful oak billiards table with its gilt panelling, rich carvings, lights, covers and even the sets of balls. It cost over £400 originally, as H. Wintle Esq of Department F5 noted with relish in his report and, being in mint condition 'would be worth just as much now'. (Nearly seventy years later this is the only Rothschild chattel that remains in the Mansion, still a cherished plaything.)

But when it came to the house itself, disapproval oozed from Wintle's pen. It was too pretentious, the rooms too large, the huge space wasted and impractical. The pillars were dismissed as imitation marble.

The truth was that Halton House was an acquisition so gigantic that bureaucratic minds boggled. With 27,000 square feet of flooring and five storeys it exceeded every normal scale laid down in Service regulations of the day. Its needs were frightening: how on earth were they to provide the 79 curbstones which the Inspector of Fire Services deemed essential for the mansion's legion of marble fireplaces? The entire Equipment Branch did not have that number in stock!

The criticisms which Halton House provoked at this time have to be seen against the desperate political circumstances surrounding the young RAF until 1925. As Chief of Air Staff, Trenchard fought one bitter engagement after another for survival; against him were ranged hostile Sea Lords, jealous Generals, parsimonious and weak Ministers and a wave of postwar pacifism.

Time and again the RAF's manpower and finances — already pared to the bone — were scrutinised by special committees which seemed bent on destroying its independence. Time and time and again the RAF's miniscule budget of under £15 million almost collapsed as it struggled to justify itself through huge peace-keeping operations in Iraq and India.

In the battle to balance the books an acquisition like Halton House looked suspiciously like a white elephant. Understandably, perhaps, Mr Wintle concluded his survey with prim comment that the mansion was 'quite unsuitable for any purpose for which the Air Ministry could use it'!

At this point the Air Council actually asked Trenchard to reconsider whether the RAF had a genuine need of the building. Trenchard himself had no doubts and he found a powerful ally in a new quarter — the vigorous Mr Winston Churchill, recently appointed to the joint post of Secretary of State for War and Air.

Churchill visited Halton on 13 April 1919, and notes made at the time show it was his opinion that 'Halton House is admirably suited as a Staff College for the Royal Air Force'. Apparently Churchill saw in Halton's pinnacles and parklands a suitable rival to the prestigious establishments of the other two Services. The plan, however, came to nothing and in 1921, after two years of argument, the Staff College found its home elsewhere.

By this time Trenchard's own vision for Halton was becoming reality; the wartime workshops so hastily erected on Alfred's pastures had developed into the largest training school for air mechanics in the world, and it was still growing.

Although Trenchard had to fight a final battle in 1921 with the Geddes Committee to save the entire station from the axe, there was no more talk of selling off the Mansion or ploughing up its velvet lawns to sow barley.

But what of Halton itself — the little village, the cluster of farms, the leafy lanes and acres of woods? Unhappily it will come as no surprise to students of Government that Alfred's model estate, which ran so smoothly when devoted to *pleasure,* virtually came apart at the seams when the Air Ministry tried to run it on bureaucratic lines.

Estate management was a nightmare for Halton's first AOC Air Commodore Francis Scarlett, and he came better qualified than most for this kind of tangle. 'Dan' Scarlett was a strict disciplinarian with an orderly mind. At Cranwell (which was a RNAS training centre before being merged in the RAF) he had won a reputation for making the large estate efficient and even profitable. But a successful encore at Halton was to elude him.

Arriving in December 1919, Scarlett soon found that the Air Council's ambitious designs had lumbered him with far more real estate than the Service needed or knew how to handle. To the fiery sea dog, hacking round the huge estate in the frosty winter afternoons, the situation was intolerable. On 4 February 1920 things came to a violent head when, booted and spurred, he clashed with a band of locals from Tring and flushed them out of the woods where they were stealing timber.

Back at his desk he wrote in fury to his masters demanding more authority. 'I feel it is my duty to bring to the notice of the Air Council the deplorable conditions of the Halton estate generally which . . . is suffering and has suffered greatly in the past from lack of local supervision. Justified discontent is rife among the tenants. The Government is being robbed continually'.

Scarlett's chief grievance was in being dogged by a bureaucratic bumbledom straight out of the pages of Swift. Although he was personally responsible to the Air Ministry for the overall management of the estate, its routine maintenance was delegated to the Lands Directorate, which also fixed the rents, arranged the leases and supervised the woodlands. Yet in 1919 that department had no permanent representative at Halton. Moreover there was constant feuding between Scarlett and the Lands Department on how much of the estate was allocated for military use and how much for producing revenue. The dispute became a scandal when Scarlett appropriated generous tracts of land for recreational purposes, including 74 acres for a golf course, which was not even a recognised Service sport!

What made this lack of control more grave was the decay into which Halton had drifted. Alfred's model estate had become, to put it bluntly, an agricultural slum. Repairs to farm buildings had ceased in 1914. Fences were down, ditches were blocked, cattle strayed and the game was poached out. Much of the grazing was so poor it was unlettable. In the woods thousands of pounds of marketable timber stood uncut or lay rotting. When the Lands Department took on timber contractors they operated without supervision and cocked a snook at their contracts.

Even Alfred's beautiful gardens around the chateau were a ruination: after four years of neglect the 40 ornamental acres and 3,000 yards of driveways and borders now resembled an Enchanted Forest.

To the Rothschild tenants the most infuriating change was the needless loss of land. The valuable fields which had been taken from them between 1914 and 1918 were still unworkable. Barbed wire, warrens of trenches and earthworks, roadways and deserted buildings (including the entire North Camp site) prevented the land from coming back into use. Yet on top of this the Lands Department — with an Olympian sense of mistiming — attempted to raise the rents in 1919. This provoked a tenant   revolt and when Winston Churchill came down in April 1919 he had to face an angry deputation.

Such Whitehall ineptitude enraged Service Officers, who had no control over the issues but had to live with the consequences. The Director of Training and Organisation came away from Halton fuming that 'The mischief done to the RAF is out of all proportion to the money gained by the Crown'.

There was worse to come. In its clumsiest dealing from this period the Lands Directorate bit the hand that had fed it in time of war. A nasty septic bite it was too, for the matter involved sewage disposal. During the war, because of the Army's problems with field hygiene. Nathaniel Charles (Lord Rothschild's son and successor) had agreed that slop water from the North Camp could be drained onto seven low-lying acres near the airfield. His tenant was not overjoyed at the sight of ablutions and cookhouse slops irrigating his grazing, but to the Rothschilds it was a reasonable sacrifice for the war effort.

For two years the waters flowed and the farmer waited patiently for restitution of the land. Then in March 1919 came a bolt from Whitehall: the Ministry commandeered 24 acres of his holding to build a permanent sewage farm for the disposal of the entire sewage (not just the slops) of RAF Halton.

The Government's behaviour in this was extremely cynical. While the Lands Directorate was outwardly quoting the 1914 Defence of the Realm regulations, the Secretary of the Air Council privately advised that 'in all probability', no right of compulsory purchase existed. (The truth of the matter was that thousands of pounds had already been spent on the site. The Government was damned if it would lose them by shifting elsewhere). It was boorish too, because the Government which had every reason for gratitude to the Rothschild family now ignored the most elementary courtesies in dealing with them. The lovely Rothschild seat at Aston Clinton, so readily loaned to the Army as divisional headquarters in 1914, was well within sniffing distance when the wind was in the west.

In vain did Rothschild lawyers argue and the family try to apply pressure at Cabinet level. Within a year the purchase was forced through at £50 an acre, and the RAF was purging its detritus on Nathaniel Charles' fields.

The significance of this shabby little Clochemerle episode is greater than it might seem. It was, after all, only five years since the English Rothschilds had entertained monarchs and presidents, helped to make or break government credit in a dozen countries, saved the good name of the City and acted as unofficial peace brokers between London and Berlin. No Minister of the Crown before 1914 would have crossed a Rothschild without the greatest circumspection. To dump sewage on his doorstep would have been political suicide.

Like so many other things in the nation's life, the war had changed all that.

As the 1920s grew older the ravages of neglect came under control. Large parts of the estate were put up for sale and territorial responsibility between the military and civilian departments clearly defined. This left the AOC with generous space for sports use and — by a curious local arrangement much in accord with Trenchard's principle of cost effectiveness — paying rent to the Air Ministry on other parts, like the airfield and golf course, used for agricultural or recreational purposes.

The financial accounts of the Station's agricultural enterprises make fascinating reading. In 1922 the AOC was responsible for a large flock of sheep, 90 pigs, seven horses, barnfuls of farming implements and vehicles and several farm labourers. His turnover was nearly £1,000 per quarter.

With these resources Scarlett and his successors tackled the outstanding problems at Halton. Much of the land used for trench warfare was ploughed over and planted with oats. Ten acres of wheat waved around the airfield and on the remainder hay was made and a polo ground laid out. Neglected pastures were earmarked for sportsfields and dressed and rolled for the first time in seven years. Football pitches, hockey pitches and cricket squares multiplied. In the summer of '22 the air was heavy with the smell of new mown hay.

Down in the village 30 acres of glass houses and vegetable gardens were still in good shape. The station went into market gardening with Alfred's former head gardener directing operations, selling not only fruit and vegetables but young trees and shrubs for planting out at other RAF establishments. Whitehall allocated special funds to restore the formal gardens and to plant some of the open spaces, which were so offensive to the Service auditors, with larch and spruce to reduce labour.

Then the forest itself began to thrive again. Between 1925 and 1930 no less than 640,000 trees were planted, over 500,000 of them from the Halton nursery. Most of these were fir and other softwood. They were a poor replacement for Alfred's murdered beechwoods, but they clothed the naked Chilterns edge and provided revenue. In 1939 most of the woodlands were taken over by the Forestry Commission.

It would be tiresome to follow the agricultural theme further. As the years passed the rural character of the station changed. Sheep gave way to gang rollers, afforestation reduced the open spaces, public rights of way were lost and service quarters sprang up in neat 'married patches' where once cattle grazed and pigs rooted.

Very properly the farming responsibilities of the station commander declined and vanished. Scarlett and his successors had done valiant work in wielding the plough as well as the sword, but they must have heaved a sigh of relief when they could return to straightforward soldiering once more.

Gilded Cage

'My argument is that war makes rattling good history and peace but poor reading'. — *Thomas Hardy.*

There is a story that on VE Day in 1945 the War Office sent out two signals. One was a general announcement of peace to all commands and the other a special explanation to RAF Halton, which never knew the war had been on.

The quip emphasised the fact that between the wars Halton was no more a typical RAF station than Halton House was a typical Service mess. The station itself was large and uncohesive. Onto the technical training school which in Trenchard's words was 'a great experiment . . . bitterly criticised at the time' was soon grafted a variety of unrelated autonomous units. These included the RAF's main hospital, its Record Office, an institute of pathology and tropical medicine, a school of cookery, an institute of hygiene and various other dental and medical establishments. (Halton's medical tradition has always been strong. During this period the Princess Mary's hospital was *inter alia* the sole RAF centre for treating venereal diseases. 'A posting to Halton' became a euphemism for something far worse).

It is not proposed to follow any of these enterprises here. The theme of this last chapter is the social ethos that surrounded Halton House and the officers who used it as their mess between the wars. The contrasts are so marked that today's officers, who are professional in their work and egalitarian in their leisure, may barely recognise Halton from the description. I can only assure them that it is derived wholly from the recollections of pre-war serving officers and contemporary records.

During the 1920s and 1930s the Officers' mess fluctuated between 70 and 100 members. Their lives were ruled by a social protocol only slightly less austere than that of a pre-1914 line regiment. Excessive deference to rank, rigid mess rules on dress and behaviour, separate dining arrangements for seniors and juniors, an insistence on calling, card leaving and other social niceties were the order of the day.

While young men might get away with a certain amount of rowdy high spirits, lapses in dress and etiquette were dealt with mercilessly. (The perilous sport of sledging down the great stairway in the dinner gong, for instance, goes right back to 1925.)

Some of the stuffiness was due to the post-Edwardian atmosphere. Mess members soon dubbed Halton House 'the Gilded Cage', and who could feel at ease in a cage with a frock-coated butler, page boys in band box hats and an ex-Rothschild steward who ran the dining room like one of Alfred's banquets? Living-in officers soon discovered another disagreeable truth about converted palaces: the comforts of a privileged few waited on hand and foot by a legion of servants did not survive when the ratio was reversed. As a new arrival wrote: 'It is hard to reconcile the lavishness and pretensions of the rest of the mess with the parlous condition wherein nobody can get a hot bath.' From the Mess Suggestion Book, 1932-58, an evocative but sparse commentary.

Alfred would have turned in his grave! (Only 80 entries were made in the first seven years, couched in terms of parliamentary politeness. Gentlemen in those days simply did not complain.)

Thanks to the Services' blinkered view of matrimony, the house was largely inhabited by young bachelors. For many years any officer rash enough to marry while under the age of 30 was penalised as a so-called 'unqualified married officer'. He was denied a right to married accommodation and marriage allowance and in many cases he had to make a decision between a Service career and his lady love.

Frustrated bachelors, however, found no comfort in the mess regulations. Ladies were not allowed inside except at specified times for tea or pre-luncheon drinks, which were served in a room set aside. Nor were there compensations of a cheerful bar for the young men. Drinking was a pastime in which gentlemen indulged *sitting down:* only horses and the lower classes drank standing. In the evenings stewards plied silver trays between a buttery and the armchairs in the grand salon.

Living-in officers were required to dine every night in Alfred's Bamfylde Room in full mess dress, the exceptions being Saturday and Sunday when they had to wear dinner jackets. By the same token married members had to dine in once a month. The mess dinners were glittering occasions, with a hundred or so officers and guests ranged down candle-lit tablets in the huge salon. Trumpeters sounded fanfares from the balcony and a military band played in the Winter Gardens. The candles flickered on white waistcoats, wing collars and mess jackets decorated with rows of Great War medals. As the port circulated, that war was refought in a haze of cigar smoke and the new one was conjured up.

Not all officers fitted into this social regime. As a contemporary put it: 'There were three types of officer in a mess of those days. Eighty per cent knew how to behave, either by breeding or study. Five per cent knew how but would not conform. Fifteen per cent did not know and would clearly never learn'.

Those exceptions were Halton's characters and misfits. They were the heroes of France, promoted for bravery in action to ranks far beyond their abilities, who lived in hope of a posting to troubled Mesopotamia or North West India. They were the nonconformists who resented the public school concept behind Trenchard's great apprentice scheme. One of them conducted an orderly room (a petty disciplinary court) with a bottle of stout on the desk, creating a scandal reminiscent of the famous Black Bottle affair at Lord Cardigan's table. They were the ex-Royal Naval Air Service officers who had fallen foul of the Sea Lords. (In 1918 they had to tie their colours to the new RAF or get out.) They still conversed in navy jargon, drank rum in the ward room and talked of shore leave to London. They were the boozers, the wounded pilots who would never fly again and other neurotic warriors coming to terms with a peacetime station with no flying role. There was an honorary mess secretary, an ex-Army lieutenant colonel, who committed suicide with his revolver in the cloakroom one day in 1930. Temporarily of unsound mind said the coroner, and there was talk of cancerphobia. But that did not stop the talk nor do the Service any good.

All in all it was no wonder that the Navy and Army looked down on the young 'Third Service', and public schools refused to regard it as a suitable career for their young gentlemen. Perhaps in self defence the theory arose that the RAF had sprung directly from the tradition of the British cavalry. (That fitted well with the image of pilots as aerial knights relying on a light hand, a good seat and nerves of steel to defeat the enemy in personal combat. The fact that most of the officers in the RFC squadrons in 1914 were from infantry regiments was overlooked). To a certain extent the authorities encouraged the chivalrous myth, and for flyers as well as non-flyers it became as important to cut a dash on a horse as to be any good at one's job.

At Halton the officers had Alfred's magnificent stables, and with an airman groom one could keep a horse on under £1 a week. The station was horse mad: there were hunters, hacks, steeplechasers and private polo ponies, as well as a string of polo ponies owned by the Saddle Club. Several officers did a bit of horse dealing on the side. The lanes of Halton were redolent with the smell of manure.

In the summer a chap could count on polo four times a week. Station fixtures were held at least once a week on the grassy expanses of the airfield. Then as now, the airfield retained the pastoral appearance of a Royal Flying Corps aerodrome with windsocks and Bessoneau canvas hangars, surrounded by pheasant coverts and plagued by crows. Before a polo fixture the pitch had to be prepared and 1,000 airmen and apprentices were marched and countermarched to flatten the turf. The other ranks did not share their officers' enthusiasm for what they irreverently called 'bleeding 'orse 'ockey'. When all was ready a signal would go off to neighbouring stations.

'ALL AEROPLANES ARE ADVISED NOT TO ATTEMPT TO LAND OR TAKE OFF'. RAF Halton was at it again.

In winter polo gave way to hunting. The 'halloo' of the Rothschild Staghounds had long since vanished from the Chilterns but the Old Berkeley and the Whaddon Chase were within hacking distance. The Old Berkeley held meets and hunt balls at Halton House down to the 1960s. On Saturdays the Tring Drag Hounds met, with the Reverend Henry Beauchamp, Halton's remarkable Irish huntin', shootin' and fishin' Catholic padre as huntsman. (Beauchamp was ex-Army and at Halton from 1919 to 1939, latterly as a Group Captain. From 1929 he was also the RAF senior Roman Catholic chaplain.) The meet was occasionally patronised by the Prince of Wales.

Hunting, polo, point-to-points, shooting, dogs, balls and receptions — for all the rigidity of the mess itself they were golden days. Duties were not arduous and there was abundant leisure time. Officially, aircrew doing ground tours were little bothered by flying, having to do a mere four hours a month to stay proficient. In fact flying was readily available and life down on the airfield was much like a free aero club. There were joy rides to sports meetings, rugby matches and reunions at other stations. Occasionally pilots overstepped the mark, as did Flying officer T.H. Nicholls one day in 1934. This young man buzzed the home of a young lady, who had confessed a partiality for sunbathing nude in the shrubberies on a hot afternoon. Nicholls' low level reconnaissance disturbed the more serious sport of the commanding officer, AVM Mac Ewen, who was shooting duck with Earl Rosebery on Tring Reservoir. He was reprimanded and given ten days' duties as orderly officer for transgressing low flying regulations. Then Mac Ewen bought him a drink in the mess.

On other occasions RAF Halton sportsmen were not averse to breaking those same regulations deliberately. Several officers rented a shoot near Pitstone and often a plane flew over to assist the partridge drives.

As the thirties advanced the atmosphere at Halton House softened. This was partly due to the liberalising influence of the civilian mess members, and partly to the high turnover of officers caused by frequent postings to the corners of the British Empire. The birds of passage included a stream of young medical officers on short courses in tropical medicine. Junior MOs are traditionally unabashed at rank and their professional scruples seldom extended to Service etiquette.

Those who stayed at Halton found it more rewarding to own or share a car than a horse. The pleasures of chukka were outweighed by those of a dash up to town to Charleston with the smart set and to motor back along empty lanes in the small hours.

In 1937 the main shortcoming of Halton House was remedied. Alfred's Winter Gardens, which for years had been a white elephant, were razed to the ground. In their place rose a three-storey block with rooms for nearly forty officers around a square quadrangle. It was architecturally unimaginative but the stone exterior, tall chimneys and high pitched roofs were sufficiently Gallic to match the main house. With the Gardens went the last of the Rothschild ghosts.

Within two years Britain was at war again and the house was swamped with conscript officers, young, clamorous and impatient for action. They created huge logistical problems for rooms, catering, heating, lighting and transport. When the war was over National Service was introduced, and the overcrowding and austerity remained so bad that a second mess opened in the former AOC's residence in the village to relieve the pressure.

For over twenty years the human tide ebbed and flowed through Halton House until National Service ended in 1961. The palmy gentlemanly days of the post-Rothschild era could never then be recaptured. At last, however, the old house was able to settle down and find a more modern, friendlier identity.

A Halton passing-out parade in the 1920s, attended by Sir Samuel Hoare, Minister for Air. AVM Lambe, Halton's diminutive AOC, is the middle officer. (RAFH)

ABOVE: Remembrance Sunday, 1927: 2,000 bareheaded airmen at RAF Halton honour the fallen of the Great War; (RAFH) BELOW LEFT: the palmy equestrian days of the 1930s. AVM MacEwen, Halton's AOC from 1931-34 and a Boer War veteran, relaxes at polo with Lady Priscilla and Catherine Willoughby. RIGHT: Polo was a leveller,

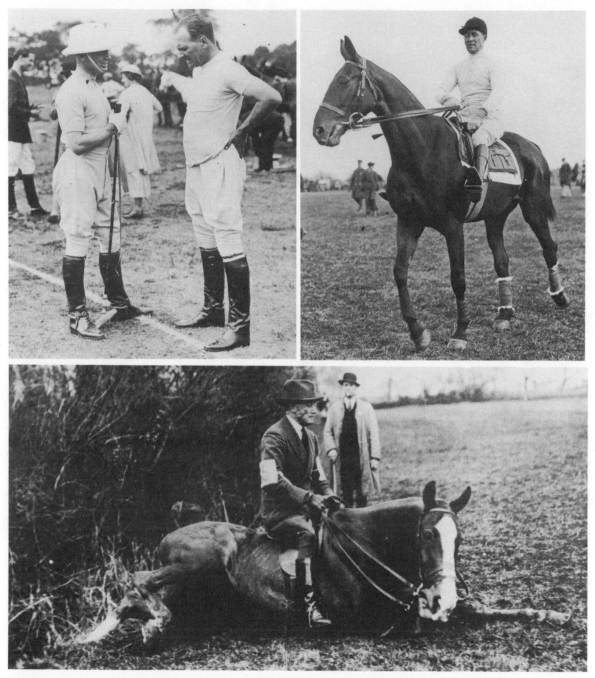

LEFT: an air commodore (right) discusses finer points of the 1934 Duke of York's
trophy with a junior officer. Senior officers frequently travelled down from London and borrowed ponies to
play at Halton; (LNAP) RIGHT: Monsignor (Group Captain) Harry Beauchamp, Halton's sporting padre from
1919-1939 and latterly the RAF's principal chaplain, winning at a point-to-point; BELOW: not so fortunate;
Padre Beauchamp takes a fall at a jumping event in the late 1930s; (RG) OPPOSITE ABOVE: archery on the
lawns outside Halton House; (TN) CENTRE: officers versus men at a 1930s Sports Day; (RAFH) BELOW: a
sample of Austin Sevens, Ford Eights and the occasional Daimler belonging to prewar officers. The Winter
Gardens (far left) were demolished in 1937. (TN)

ABOVE: A summer show down on the airfield in the 1930s. These events were the forerunners of RAF Halton's successful modern Open Days. The 'buildings' are elaborate frame tents erected by local businessmen; (JM) BELOW: the sombre appearance of Alfred's billiards room decorated with trophies of the Raj and club furniture. (HH)

Centennial

The Royal Air Force station at Halton came through the 1939-45 war unscathed: it suffered two harmlessly jettisoned bombs, one of which took several days to find in the undergrowth.

Since then the station has flourished; churches, schools, offices, messes, gymnasia, housing and new hospital and dental facilities have been built. The investment of millions of pounds has wedded the RAF indissolubly to Halton.

Over the same period the authorities have sold off the Rothschild heritage of houses and land, often with more thought for the present than the future. Speculative builders have filled the vacuum with houses far beyond the pockets of the military. Halton village, once a quiet RAF annexe, has become a dormitory village for commuters.

Amidst all this 20th century development stands Alfred's magnificent anachronism. Many see it, as did the Ministry men in 1918, as a gigantic white elephant ruinous to heat and keep in good order and chronically short of the right kind of accommodation. Abandon it, cry the critics, and let us have something functional in chrome and concrete. Sell it to the Arabs (what a splendid casino!).

Such arguments overlook the unique character of Halton House. Rightly or wrongly it enjoys an aura and a tradition which are not found in any other RAF establishment. It is also fortunately a listed building whose architectural appeal can only increase with time. At the time of writing (one hundred years after the house was completed) a modest modernisation scheme is in hand. Far more expenditure will be necessary and, as the chateau moves into its second hundred years, one hopes that its fate will be decided by wiser heads than those which demolished the lovely Aston Clinton mansion, or compelled the great art heritage at Mentmore Towers to be dismembered for death duties.

One hundred years ago a vision haunted Baron Ferdinand de Rothschild concerning his beloved creation, Waddesdon Manor:

'May the day be yet distant when weeds will spread over the garden, the terraces crumble into dust, the pictures and cabinets cross Channel or the Atlantic and the melancholy cry of the night jar sound from the deserted towers'.

Halton has long since lost its own art treasures: Heaven preserve it from the cry of the night jar.

APPENDIX A

Origins of the House of Rothschild

The fortunes of the early Rothschilds are well covered in the existing histories of the family. Only a brief summary is given here.

Their rise to fame began in Frankfurt-on-Main in the Principality of Hesse Cassel in the second half of the 18th century. Frankfurt was a great trading centre, dealing in numerous European currencies and offering Jews some degree of protection. Here in 1763 came young Amschel Mayer Rothschild (1744-1812), whose Jewish name derived from (the house of) the Red Shield. A ghetto boy from Hanover, he was orphaned by smallpox at the age of eleven and started trading in a small way in rare coins.

In Frankfurt he gained the numismatic interest of William the Landgrave (later the Elector) of Hesse-Cassel, one of the richest and greediest princes in Europe.

The French Revolution and the Napoleonic Wars brought 25 years of ferment to central Europe, with acute shortages of money, materials and men. The Elector did disgustingly well by 'trafficking in valour', ie hiring out his own soldiers to one side (the French) and lending the profits from the transaction to their enemies. Amschel flourished with him, dealing in scarce commodities, exchanging currencies and money bills and finally handling the Elector's own massive transactions. When Napoleon finally drove the shiftless ruler out in 1807, Amschel was the sole custodian of his fabulous hidden funds. While staying essentially loyal to his master, he used his opportunities most richly.

Meanwhile the real Rothschild wealth — Amschel's five talented sons — were deployed over Europe as his agents in England, France, Austria, Germany and Italy. By a mixture of excellent communications, rapid shifting of assets and clannish secrecy they beat Napoleon's agents at their own game time and again.

The most successful was the second son Nathan (1777-1836) who founded the English branch of the family. He arrived in Manchester in 1800 with £10,000 in his pocket, made a killing in cotton and moved rapidly into bullion in London.

In 1810 he snapped up £800,000 of gold (using money borrowed from the Elector's exchequer) from the East India Company and made another fortune reselling it to the British Government. The Government was desperate to get gold safely to the Duke of Wellington in Portugal to keep the Peninsular campaign going. Obligingly Nathan also undertook this transaction.

With astonishing cheek he sent the gold openly to his brother James in Paris, who actually persuaded the French that it was part of an elaborate scheme to bankrupt the British Government! Later the money was smuggled overland to Portugal in cases of old clothes.

Through this and other daring adventures the Rothschilds emerged in 1815 as the richest banking family in Europe, with assets of £50 million. They were even powerful enough to oblige the Habsburgs to grant them a coat of arms, which incorporated the famous five arrows for the five sons, and five hereditary baronies.

For years the English branch of the family, represented by the banking house of N.M. Rothschild and Sons, was the cornerstone of the family's European network. Nathan dominated it with broken English, boorish manners and brilliant acumen until his death in 1836.

By now the threads of the family were beginning to separate. The Buckinghamshire story begins with his four sons, Lionel (1808-79), Anthony (1810-76), Nathaniel (1812-70) and Mayer (1818-74).

APPENDIX B

Officers commanding RAF Halton, 1919-1939

RAF Halton between the wars was an important command. Its Commanding Officers were all of air (ie general) rank and many went on to hold even higher Commands. These gentlemen were a spirited and salty bunch. No less than five of the eight had been former Royal Naval Air Service pilots. It would be a shame if one day their names were remembered at Halton only through some dreary eponymous camp roadways.

1919-1924. AVM Francis Rowland Scarlett was the first of the naval aviators. Born in 1875, he went through Dartmouth, was commissioned sublieutenant in 1895 and served in the Boer War. He took his flying certificate in 1913 and, after a brief spell aboard the ill fated *HMS Hermes* (see below), was given the key appointment in charge of the RNAS headquarters at Sheerness with the title of Inspecting Captain of Aircraft. He was responsible for assembling all the Navy's aircraft at the great Spithead review in 1914. As ICA he was so dogmatic and forceful that the letters were popularly interpreted as meaning 'I Can't Agree'.

He saw service in the Eastern Mediterranean and was awarded the DSO after leading a joint bombing raid with Colonel George Dawson, RFC. They ran into a German fighting formation and fought it 'with not so much as a pistol on board'. Not surprisingly their airplane crashed on return.

Scarlett transferred to the RAF in 1918 with the rank of Air Commodore. After Halton he went to Venice in 1927 with the RAF High Speed Flight which won the coveted Schneider trophy. He commanded RAF Middle East in 1929, retired in 1931 and died in 1934.

1924-1928. AVM Charles Laverock Lambe was another sea-going officer before turning aviator. In 1914 he commanded the antique twin screw cruiser *Hermes* (1894), recently converted to carry three seaplanes. He was torpedoed within sight of Dunkirk in 1914; a contemporary writer remarked that but for the lamentable loss of life the sinking of HMS *Hermes* was not regretted!

Lambe took his flying certificate in 1915, joined the RNAS, and for much of the war commanded the important RNAS station at Dunkirk. After the war he was Director of Equipment at the Air Ministry, and after Halton he commanded Coastal Command until he retired in 1931.

He died in 1953 after 22 years of quiet retirement in the country. His obituarist (with a studied disregard for Lambe's RAF career) recorded in the *Aeroplane* that 'Charles Lambe was the sort of naval officer of the type which has made the Navy what it is'!

1928-1931. The early career of Air Commodore Ian Malcolm Bonham-Carter, the one-legged Northumberland Fusilier, is outlined in Chapter 9. After the Great War he was appointed to command No 11 (Irish) Group. When Sinn Feiners stole his staff car during 'the Troubles', the remarkable man commandeered another vehicle, caught them up and, furiously brandishing his crutch, recovered the Government's property.

On return to England he went to the RAF Depot at Uxbridge, famous for its efficiency, discipline and smart drill. Later he was Air Commodore commanding No 3 Group, just as parachutes were coming into use. Bonham-Carter, who always led from in front, insisted on making a jump himself in spite of his handicap.

His first appointment to Halton was considered an excellent choice: 'His organising ability, experience and strict sense of ability helped firmly to lay the foundations of the great school'. His second tenure at Halton was marred by the tragic death of his 17-year-old son in a firearm accident in 1930. The shock, together with the constant pain of his war injury, led to his retirement in 1931. He returned on the outbreak of war and served with distinction at Fighter Command HQ during the Battle of Britain. He died at Princess Mary's Hospital in 1954, aged 71.

1931-1934. AVM Sir Norman Duckworth Kerr MacEwen had already passed his apogee before coming to Halton. Born in 1881, he was an Argyll and Sutherland Highlander who won the Queen's Medal with five clasps in the Boer War. He joined the RFC as major in 1916 and took his flying certificate in the same year. He served in Iraq during the War and from 1919 as C-in-C RAF India. He was subsequently commandant of the Central Flying School, where his rule was described as 'a charming mingling of benignity and discipline'. After Halton he retired because of ill-health and died at RAF Hospital Uxbridge in 1953, aged 72.

1935-1936. Air Commodore John Tremayne Babington had only an 18-month sojourn at Halton. Born in 1891, he went through Osborne and Dartmouth and was gazetted midshipman in 1908. As Sub-Lt Babington he had the credit of piloting the first successful British wireless trials at sea in May 1913, transmitting up to 45 miles from a Short seaplane.

He was one of the original twelve flight commanders of the RNAS, and one of three naval pilots who, in late 1914, flew their frail Avro machines with 80-HP Gnome engines on an amazing bombing raid into Germany. They flew from Belfort on a crooked course (avoiding Switzerland) to bomb the Zeppelin sheds at Friedrichshaven. Years later the historian Sir Walter Raleigh wrote: 'There have since been many longer and greater raids but this flight of 250 miles into gunfire, in the frail Avro with its humble horse power, can compare as an achievement with the best of them'. Babington was awarded the DSO and created Chevalier of the Legion d'Honneur. In 1918 he transferred to the RAF as Squadron Leader. After the war he had several important staff and command posts, including air representative to the League of Nations for five years. After his Halton command he rose to Air Marshal and was knighted in 1942. He led the unsuccessful RAF mission to Moscow in 1943 and retired in 1944, settling in Cornwall. Here he assumed his mother's maiden name, which was well known locally, by deed poll. As Sir John Tremayne he was appointed Sheriff of Cornwall in 1954 and died in 1979 at the age of 87.

1936-1938. Air Commodore George Ranald Macfarlane Reid was born in 1893 and like MacEwen, was an Argyll and Sutherland Highlander. He joined up in 1914, was seconded next year to the RFC and served in France. After the war he spent some time in Egypt and the Sudan before proceeding as air attache to Washington. He was Air Commodore during his two years at Halton and rose to AVM, to command RAF Aden (1938-41) and later RAF West Africa (1943-46). He was knighted in 1945 but, like others, he fell victim to post-war cuts and was retired prematurely in 1946.

1938-1939 and 1940-1942. Air Commodore George Bentley Dacre was twice AOC at Halton. Born in 1891, he was educated at Clifton and Bristol University where he read engineering, and took his flying certificate as early as 1911.

He joined the RNAS as a probationary sublieutenant in August 1914 and saw a great deal of fighting in the eastern Mediterranean, winning the DSO over Gallipoli. He had the distinction of sinking a Turkish vessel while taxying towards it under rifle fire! This unconventional engagement was one of the first sinkings achieved with aerial torpedo. The Turks got their own back when the Arabs captured him in 1916, and Dacre spent the rest of the war as a POW.

He held various commands and special posts between the wars, including head of the British air mission to Greece in 1929 and air attache in Rome in 1935-37. His first spell at Halton was interrupted by the outbreak of war, and he was appointed to command the Advanced Air Striking Force of ten bomber squadrons. But things went badly, his appointment was downgraded, and he was back at Halton within the year. He was compulsorily retired before the war ended, retired to Sussex and died at Rottingdean in January 1962.

1939-1940. The last of this colourful era, AVM Sir Oliver Swann, was appointed to command Halton only a few days before Hitler invaded Poland. Swann was also the last in the tradition of Edwardian naval aviators. Born in 1878 with the family name of Schwann, he passed through Dartmouth and was promoted sublieutenant in 1898.

Long before the navy took up aviation, Swann was an enthusiastic amateur. He bought an early Avro biplane for £700, fitted it with prototype floats, and managed to become the first British aviator to take off from salt water. It was a fitting achievement for an RN officer, even though the short flight (at Barrow-in-Furness) ended in a watery belly-flop.

Soon after the outbreak of the Great War, he had a narrow escape when flying a German Mars aircraft which the RNAS had purchased for comparison purposes. With another officer, he was forced to put down on Scarborough race course, where they were immediately surrounded by a band of suspicious and trigger-happy army recruits. The combination of their unfamiliar blue uniforms, the German markings on their fuselage and the Germanic-sounding name of 'Commander Oliver Schwann' on the senior officer's papers nearly got them shot out of hand. Only the timely arrival of another RNAS officer saved them.

Not long after that event Schwann changed his name! In 1915, as Captain Swann, he commanded HMS *Campania,* a 20,000 ton Cunarder refitted as an aircraft carrier to take a dozen float planes. In 1918 he transferred to the RAF and — by a typical quirk of the period — was for a time Deputy Chief of Air Staff, with the rank of Brigadier General, before changing hats and going to Malta as an Air Commodore. He returned to be Member for Personnel on the Air Council and finished his career commanding RAF Middle East from headquarters in Cairo. He retired in 1929 but returned to harness to take the Halton command during the difficult year 1939-40. He died at Guildford in 1948.

Bibliography

Asquith, Herbert H. *Memories and Reflections 1852-1927* (1928).

Battersea, Lady Constance. *Reminiscences* (1922).

Carnarvon, Earl of. *No Regrets* (1976).

Chamber's *The Book of Days* (1863).

Corti, Baron Egon. *The Rise of the House of Rothschild* (1928).

Cowles, Virginia. *The Rothschilds, a Family of Fortune* (1979).

Curzon, Colin. *Flying Wild* (1941).

Cutlack F.M. *Official History of Australia in the War of 1914-1918* (1923).

Davis, Charles. *A Description of the Works of Art Forming the Collection of Alfred de Rothschild* (1884).

Davis, Richard W. *Political Change and Continuity, 1760-1885. A Buckinghamshire Study* (1972).

East, Sir Ronald. *A South Australian Colonist of 1836 and his Descendants* (1972).

Franklin, Jill. *The Gentleman's Country House and its Plan 1835-1914* (1981).

Fowler, J.K. *Echoes of Old County Life* (1892).
        Recollections of Old Country Life (1894).

Gibbs, Robert G. *History of Aylesbury* (1885, reprinted 1971).

Girouard, Marc. *The Victorian Country House* (1971).

Greville, Countess Frances. *Afterthoughts* (1931).

Haydock, Grace. *Halton House* (revised 1981).

Hobhouse, Hermione. *Thomas Cubitt, Master Builder* (1971).

Jones, H.A. *The War in the Air* (1928 et seq).

Kerr, Robert. *The Gentleman's House, or How to Plan English Residences from the Parsonage to the Palace* (1864).

Kimber, Charles T. *Son of Halton* (1977).

Langtry, Emily C. *The Life of Mrs Langtry, the Jersey Lily* (1925).

Langtry, Lily. *Days I Knew* (1925).

Lipscomb, *The History and Antiquities of the County of Buckinghamshire* (1847).

Moneyppenny, W.P. *Life of Benjamin Disraeli* (1912).

Morton, Frederic. *The Rothschilds, a Family Portrait* (1962).

Parrott, Hayward. *Aylesbury Vale Yesterdays* (1981).

Pevsner, Sir Nikolaus. *The Buildings of England (Buckinghamshire)* (1960).

Priest, John. *Agricultural Survey of the County* (1813).

Roth, Cecil. *The Magnificent Rothschilds* (1939).

Sandilands, H.R. *The Fifth in the Great War* (1938).

Scott, Clement. *Old Days in Bohemian London* (1919).

Sheahan, J.J. *History and Topography of Buckinghamshire* (1862).
Snow, R.S. *History of Wendover* (1972).
Victoria County History (1908).
West, Sir Algernon. *Private Diaries of Sir Algernon West, GCB* (1922).

Manuscript or private papers consulted for this study include the Dashwood papers (Bodleian Library and Bucks County Records Office), various other public papers at the County Records Office, the private papers of Private Arthur Patrick and of Wing Commander S. E. Townson. Other sources are acknowledged in the text.

Periodicals and newspapers consulted include: *The Architect, The Aeroplane, Bucks and Berks Countryside, Bucks Free Press, Bucks Herald, Bucks Life, The Builder, Country Life, Halton Magazine, Wendover Gazette,* and *The Times.*

Official and semi-official Service sources consulted include: Halton House Mess Committee records, RAF Halton station records, RAF officers' Records of Service, Army and Air Ministry files in the Public Records Office, *A Short History of the RAF* (1929), The Composition of Headquarters (a monthly wartime listing of appointments and unit locations in the UK).

Directories consulted include: Burke's *Peerage,* the *Dictionary of National Biography,* Kelly's *Directory* and *British Sports and Sportsmen Past and Present* (1908).

Index

Key to Caption Credits

AA	Author
BCRL	Bucks County Reference Library
EB	E.J.G. Bowden
BC	B.M. Coe
KD	K.M. Dunbar
RE	Sir R. East
RG	R.G. Grace
HA	Haltonian Association
HH	Halton House Mess Collection
AK	A. Kirsop
MK	M. Knock

EL	E.M. Lancaster
JM	J.M. MacMillan
NMR	National Monuments Record
TN	T.H.L. Nicholls
LNAP	London News Agency Photos
SP	S.J. Power
MoD	Ministry of Defence
HP	H. Parrott
RAFH	RAF Halton collection
ER	E. Robinson
ES	E. Sanders

Subscribers

Presentation Copies

1 Halton House Officers' Mess
2 Halton Village and Parish
3 Mr Edmund de Rothschild
4 RAF Halton Station Headquarters
5 The Trenchard Library
6 Wendover Library
7 Aylesbury Library
8 Aylesbury Vale District Council
9 R.G. Grace
10 AVM J.N.C. Cooke
11 Norman Chandler

12 Andrew & Jacqui Adam
13 Clive & Carolyn Birch
14 Dr Roger Highfield
15 Robert Adam
16 Katherine Adam
17 Elizabeth Adam
18 Wg Cmr C.J. McCluskey
19 Rev G. Robson
20 Wg Cmr M. Mahoney
21 RAF Medical Library, Halton
22 Flt Lt P.L. Weller
23 Flt Lt D. Warneford
24 Sqn Ldr J. Green
25 Flt Lt K.G. Baylis
26
27 Gp Capt R.F. Brown
28 Gp Capt A.J.C. Balfour
29 Sqn Ldr W.R. Collins RAF (Retd)
30 P.J. Mastin
31 Mrs Olive Cameron
32 Wg Cmr G.S. Wilson
33 Sqn Ldr J.B. Kershaw
34
35 Wg Cmr R.J. Lane
36 Peter Chard
37 Sqn Ldr N. Holden
38 Victoria & Albert Museum
40 Flt Lt V.D. Goodridge
41 Flt Lt A.D. Rainbow
42 Flt Lt A.S. Haslam
43 Sqn Ldr J. Jones
44 Wg Cmr W.V. Holden
45 Sqn Ldr M.N. James
46 Sqn Ldr V. Escott
48 Sqn Ldr R.E. Tettmar
49 Sqn Ldr A.J. Green
50 AVM J.N.C. Cooke
51 Gp Capt J.K. Cloherty

52 Flt Lt Scott
53 G.A. Tyson
54 Wg Cmr Anthony Campbell
55 Dr B.H. Newman
56
   Flt Lt M.C.R. Stamford
58
59 S.D. Arthur
60 Gp Capt D.E. Dormer
61 Flt Lt E.M. Lyttle
62 Sqn Ldr Cave
63 Flt Lt C. Cordery
64 Flt Lt R.J.R. Smart
65 Wg Cmr A. Stephens
66 Flt Lt M.A. Taylor
67 Sqn Ldr A.I. Attwood
68 Fg Off P.C. Lyons
69 Mrs B.E. Tettmar
70 Mrs Joan Hurry
71 Mr & Mrs P. Jaffray
72 Wg Cmr David J. Rainford
73 C. Wakefield
74 Fg Off S. Huxtable-Selly
75 Sqn Ldr C. Palmer
76 Wg Cdr J.V. Emery
77 Sqn Ldr J.A. Kay
78 Air Cmre A.J. Clegg RAF (Retd)
79 Sqn Ldr M.K. Marshall
80 Flt Lt B. Quarman
81 Flt Lt M.A. Ashton
82 Wg Cmr J.A. Rowlands
83 Flt Lt I.J. Cromarty
84 Flt Lt K.R. Watson
85 Flt Lt & Mrs K.F. Dyson
86 Flt Lt P. Upfold
87 Dr K.E. Underwood Ground
88 P.A. Edney

89 Wg Cmr G.J. Beveridge
90 Flt Lt G.A. Jermy
91 K. Kirsop
92 D. Wilcox
93 Flt Sgt C. Payne
94 E.W. Marsden
95
96 Flt Sgt F.N. Slingsby
97 AVM J.M. Jones
98 Gp Capt J. Mackey
99 Gp Capt R.O. Bater (Retd)
100 Officer Commanding RAF Halton
101 Flt Lt A. Brown
102 T.N.N. Grose
103 Padre M.J. Hill RAF VRT
104 Air Cmre B.W. Opie
105 Sqn Ldr A.D. Walker
106 Mrs B. Coe
107 Flt Sgt Ernest Poole
108 Mrs M. Diston
109 S.G. Stentiford
110 Sgt. G. Owen
111 J. Blakey
112 Flt Lt D.R. Tucker
113 Mrs Joan Reynolds
114 Mrs M. French
115 D. Warham
116 F.P. Waterson
117 N. Prendergast
118 Sgt T. Vaughan
119 Flt Sgt R.C. Oxbury
120 D.J. Mummery
121 D. Wareham
122 L.F. Mortimer
123 Sgt P.R. Irvine
124 Flt Sgt Taylor
125 Flt Sgt A.P. Winfield
126 Mrs Jane Cooper

127 Albin John Reed
128 Mrs D.E.M. Ratcliffe
129 Mrs C.J. Atkins
130 Mr & Mrs T.A. Harris
131 R.J. Shripton
132 Mrs M. Armitage
133 W.E. Collier
134 Mrs G.M. Jackman
135 Mrs L.M. Roques
136 Ms G. Headland
137 E.R. Cook
138 Mrs M. McMorland
139 William Slade
140 Miss Eileen Robinson
141 Fred Sanders
142 Tom Benson
143 Mr & Mrs Tom Blundell
144 Mr & Mrs R. Langdon
145 Peter Hawkins
146 David Bullock
147 Mr & Mrs V.J. Dean
148 Miss Sally Cameron
149 Miss Sylvia Challis
150 Dr & Mrs Kenneth H. Mueller
151 Dr & Mrs Lee K. Hermann
152 Mr & Mrs G. Williams
153 Wg Cmr & Mrs John Gearing
154 Wg Cmr & Mrs Richard Howell
155 Mr & Mrs G.A. Brasted
156 E.G. Kemp
157 Flt Lt & Mrs A. Pooley
158 A.M. Gillespie
159 Douglas & Lorna Lang
160 Sqn Ldr & Mrs Robin Dugdale
161 Mrs Marian Bew

162 Mrs Barbara McElney
163
164 George Brodie
165 Mr & Mrs Terence Johnson
166 Roger Collins
167 Miss K.M.D. Dunbar
168 Lt Col & Mrs John George
169 Dr Malcolm Philips
170
171 Wg Cmr & Mrs D.E. Larkin
172 Mrs J. Muston
173 B.M. Pratt
174 M.G. Champion
175 R.T. Rossiter
176 Mrs M.A.C. Etchells
177 Colin & Zena Bridger
178 Buckinghamshire
179 County Library
180 Flt Lt C.A. Maple
181 Brian & Maria Gibbins
182 Dr R.F. Bury
183 W.F. Leyman
184 Thomas F. McCosh
185 William D. Thomson
186 Lewis Jones
187 Kitty Ballinghall
188 Wg Cmr Brian I. Mason OBE RAF
189 Education Officer RAF Stafford
190 D.H. Kitching
191 T.J. Laundy
192 Humphrey & Company Wingrave
193 Flt Lt J. Waddington
194 A.C. Marsh
195 Wg Cmr Trevor Taylor
196 St John Red Cross Dept, RAF Halton
197 Elizabeth Wykes
198 Hobbs
199 Dr Derek Parkin
200 Dr T.J. Betteridge
201 Station Education & Training Officer, RAF High Wycombe
202 Station Education & Training Officer, RAF Wattisham
203 RAF, Aldergrove
204 Dr J.W. Culver-James
205 John Camp JP
206 Peter Sharp
207
208 The Trenchard
209 Library
210 Gordon Bailey
211 Gp Cpt M.J. Evans
212 Sqn Ldr C. Ellam
213 D.G. White
214
215 T.D. McCluskey

216 F.G.F. Bevis
217 Mrs G.J. Betteridge
218
219 Don Bell
2210 Aylesbury Grammar School
221 Arthur Taylor
222 The Library, John Colet School, Wendover
223 OC FECTS RAF St Atham
224 Mrs G.V. Elliott
225 Alan Kirkpatrick
226 M.W. Rodger
227 Station Education Officer, RAF Swanton Morley
228 C.D. Williams
229 Mary Perry
230 Wg Cmr J.B. Yates
231 RAF Boulmer
232 B.M. Stevens
233
234 Monica Harries
235 Peter Locke
236 Stephen George Williams
237 W.G. Dawson
238 John P. O'Hara
239 J.K. Mason
240 RAF Brampton
241 Peter Cannon
242 Flt Lt M.J.G. & Mrs. J. Watkins
243 Ruth Osborn-Smith
244 Senior Education & Training Officer, RAF Kinloss
245 Flt Lt W.M. Aitken
246 Mrs J.M. Snelling
247 Dr P.J. Stevens OBE
248 Mr.& Mrs S. Terry
249 RAF Valley
250 Wg Cmr M.J. Uglow RAF (Retd)
251 Wg Cmr R.T. Lang
252 W. Watson
253 F.D. Clarke
254 Sqn Ldr J. Clementson
255 K. Holliday
256 Colin R. Raynor
257 Carole & John Christie
258 S. Perry
259 Wg Cmr J.W. Higgins RAF (Retd)
260 A. Greenacre
261 O.L.J. Carley
262 James R. Brooker
263 Eric Yeadon
264 W.D. Grant
265 Sqn Ldr V.G. Spalding RAF (Retd)
266 AVM Sir Ralph Jackson

267 D. Jeremy
268 Wg Cmr & Mrs C.E. Castle
269 M.D. Berry
270 Gp Capt L.J. Jenkins OBE
271 M. J. Goakes
272 Wg Cmr C.J.T. Coombs
273 North Denes Aerodrome Ltd
274 L.W. Clark
275 Lien Esaw
276 Bernard R. Pumfrey
277 Miss G. Scarr
278 J. Bushby
279 Dr I. Chorlton
280 Wg Cmr S.A. Cullen
281 Flt Sgt T.M. Bastick BEM
282 Sir Ronald East
283 H.R. French
284 J.W. Watson
285 W.J. Hughes
286 Sqn Ldr D.M.D. Tungate
287 D.W. Pearse
288 Dr M.A. Salmon
289 Joan MacMillan
290 Sqn Ldr & Mrs K.R. Jackson
291 Air Cmre G.V. Lobley
292 C.B.R. Garner
293 Desmond Keen
294 Berkshire County Library
295 A. Wardell
296 J.H. Iddes
297 A.D. Dorsett
298 Gp Capt T.W.P.
299 Clifford
300 L.C. Ozouf
301 Wg Cmr F.J. Moden
302 Flt Lt S.J. Duncan MA WRAF
303 H.R. Sutton
304 Sqn Ldr Robert Semple
305 A.R.J. Thorogood
306 Ernest William Young
307 R.F. Chiverton
308 John Geeves
309 Harry Horton
310 M.B. Simmons
311 Pat Barlow
312 John I. Farman
313 S. Davies
314 L.A. Savigar
315 R.H. Palmer
316 H. Binks
317 Eric Townley
318 J.H. Ramsden
319 Alfred Bunn
320 Robert Charles Davey
321 Wg Cmr R.E. Bracher

322 David Forbes Waddell
323 W.J. Brain
324 P.J. Bridle
325 G. Howard
326 W.H.J. Davis
327 Harold Wanstall
328 F.W. Barkes
329 Gp Capt E.T.J. Manning
330 R.J.N. MacLachlan
331 R. Inglis
332 Wg Cmr S.C. Kearn
333 Euros Williams
334 R.H. Bailey
335 Frederick Mason
336 G.L. Harding
337 Clive Wilson
338 Arthur F. Willis
339 C.P. Stephenson
340 Mrs Margaret Aitchison
341 Dennis Tebbutt
342 R.R. Brooks
343 Wg Cmr A.H.C. Markey
344 H.G. Simpson
345 F. Merrien
346 J.T. Jeffery
347 Ian N. Macrae
348 B.W. Brennan
349 The Librarian, Bucks Archaeological Society
350 F.C. Haines
351 A.E. Shilton
352 Francis William Payne
353 M.H. Chapple
354 Sqn Ldr J.L. Alton
355 J.W. Ireland
356 Arthur Severn
357 J.E. Anderson
358 C.R. Hartnell
359 A.E. Sweetman
360 T.H. Collett
361 R. Burns
362 R. West
363 Walter Rimmer
364 L.J.M. Parry
365 David A. Price
366 Mrs Wynne Maw
367 Christopher Russ
368 Mrs Edgerton
369 Dr A. Hogarth
370 E.D. Artus
371 Reg Wilkinson
372 T.S. Harrison MBE
373 Jack Anstess
374 L.C.S. Warwick
375 'Chaka' Webster
376 P.F. Catling
377 J.R. Frapwell
378 Anthony C.J. Hill
379 C.G. Stallwood
380 Gp Capt K.J.B. Dunlop
381 G.A. Horward
382 Fred Clayton
383 Wg Cmr D.T. Brown

384 E.W. Whitley
385 Thomas Danford Plumbe
386 May S. Letch
387 W.F. Riley
388 D.R. Baum
389 Flt Lt R.C. Mitchell
390 Philip W. Rodman
391 R.H. Syrett
392 R.C. Bowers
393 Duncan R. Goodacre
394 S. Bruce
395 W.S. Hayes
396 R.G.O. Hawes
397 S.F. Tillman
398 Keith John Day
399 P.N. Kingwill
400 C.J. Butler
401 Robert Hillson Poynton
402 John E. Mackie
403 Philip John Hile
404
405 Norman F. Johnston
406 Robert Samuel
407 Peter Dunstan
408 J.F. Collier
409 J.A.S. Ackerman
410 F.J.W. Foskett
411 G.E. Perrett
412
414 Mrs Jenny Truelove
415 D.T. Whinyates
416 N.G. Brace
417 Mrs Edna Adam
418 S.M. Newman
419 Andrew Irvine
420 K.B. Smith
421 Gp Capt J.C. Ainsworth
422 Foster Robson
423 C.A. Robinson
424 John H. Cook
425 S.R. Ackroyd

426 Capt D.J. Stuart
427 Terence O'Halloran
428 L.J. Neaves
429 A.T. Bint
420 V. Kynaston
431 Maurice Short
432 Peter R.P. Walton
433 Earl of Ilchester
434 Michael J.S. Roberts
435 Peter Brewster
436 V.M.E. Denham
437 Alex Lindsay
438 A. Brian J. Bamforth
439 Donald Wares
440 John Trevor Prentice
441 H.W. Van Lokven
442 Josephine M. Midgley
443 Anthony Lark
444 Sqn Ldr D.H.A. Skillings
445 H.D. Judkins
446 B.E. Edwards
447 Gp Capt L.J. Bristow MBE RAF (Retd)
448 Gordon H.G. Ogden
449 G.V.R. Jones OBE RAF (Retd)
450 G.E.T. Mulligan
451 John Haines
452 F. Crowther
453 F.G. Hart
454 Gp Capt Mahaddie
455 Duncan Allison
456 H.L. Martin
457 H.J. Swain
458 S. Kingsbury
459 Laurence Rasmussen
460 L.F. Barker
461 Robert Horn
462 John Goates
463 Colin Walter Thomas
464 J.P. Kellett
471 A.E.W. Field

465 Gp Capt Ivor F. Easton
466 J. Cornick
467 Martin Curtis
468 R.B. Loader
469 P.N. Sherwood
470 J.E. Kelt
472 Air Cmre R.J. Offord
473 C.V. Davies
474 Wg Cmr A. Ransford MBE RAF (Retd)
475 Thomas Alexander
476 T.M. Hughes
477 F.W.J. Hain
478 J. Pearson
479 S.C.V. Chiswell
480 J.B. Fitzpatrick
481 Michael Armitage
482 Bruce P. Rowden
483 D.J. Silver
484 J.W. MacFarlane MM
485 David H. Pattison
486 P.B. Sheppard
487 Flt Lt B.J. Down (Retd)
488 F.H. Harman
489 Richard Butler
490 F.E. Saunders
491 C. Base
492 B.G. Mercer
493 Graham Scott
494 G.C. Bass
495 Sqn Ldr C.J.M. Chilcott RAF (Retd)
496 Frank Charles Cox
497 John Lapsley
498 R.A. Jones
499
500 W.R. Greenwood
501 R. Allen
502 Fred Mallon
503 J.G. Berry
504 Richard A. Lea
505 W.J. Taylor
506 R.S. Conduit

507 Mrs Betty Roberts
508 Mrs M. Jenkins
509 Miss A.M. Kelly
510 J.C. Monk
511 R.J. Surfleet
512 Mrs B. Illidge
513 Mrs Kirsop
514 Mrs Maureen Knock
515 Mrs L.M. Brierton
516 Mrs M.J. Blunden
517 Robert William Kent
518 A.K. Potter
519 N.G. Chorlton
520 Miss M. Sale
521 Frank Cregan
522 L.J. Booker
523 K.W. Beattie
524 Charles Bray
525 Professor & Mrs Gwyn Jones
526 David Leo Haines
527 R.J. Surfleet
528 G.W. Vidgen
529
530 Dr John Christie
531 Buckinghamshire
532 County Library
533 R.M. Scott
534 Derrick C. Hibbard
535 Dennis Willis
536 Eric R.J. Wythe
537 Eric Morton Stevens
538 J.F. Van Der Wateren
539 Colin Clive Baldwin
540 H.D. Nicholls
541 C.W. Clark
542 A.J. Atkinson
543 Dr John Smith
544 Sqn Ldr W. Fell
545 David J. Symonds
546 Douglas F. Meacock
547 Sq Ldr J.W. Wilson MBE RAF (Retd)

Remaining names unlisted

131

Long Copse

Furze Covert

Lakefield Covert

Rosemead Covert

Marl Copse

Gas Works

Lower Farm

School

St. Michael's Church
(Rectory)

Halton

Halton Cottage

WESTON TURVILLE PH.

GRAND JUNCTION CANAL

Surveyed in 1877.   Revised in 1898.
Reprint 90/98 Re-Levelled 1898.

CHARACTERISTICS AND SYMBOLS FOR BOUNDARIES, &c.

Printed and Published by the Director General at the

County		Municipal Wards	C
	County	Urban Districts	U
Boroughs	Parliamentary	Civil Parishes	P
	Municipal	Rural Districts	R